Reflexpower™
for WILLPOWER ALTERNATIVE

Reflexpower™ *for* WILLPOWER ALTERNATIVE

Coping with Coronavirus

Reflexpower™ Behavioral Strategy is a
Certifiable New Alternative to Self-Control Willpower

Bill Wilson

Copyright © 2020 by Bill Wilson.

All rights reserved. This book or any portion thereof may not be reproduced or used in any manner whatsoever without the express written permission of the publisher except for the use of brief quotations in a book review.

Reflexpower™ is a trademark for the *Reflexpower*™ book series.

Cover Design by Berge Design

ISBN: 978-0-578-70170-7 (ebook)
ISBN: 978-0-578-71226-0 (paperback)

Scripture taken from the NEW AMERICAN STANDARD BIBLE®
Copyright © 1960, 1962, 1963, 1968, 1971, 1972, 1973, 1975, 1977, 1995 by The Lockman Foundation. Used by permission.

Contents

The Reflexpower™ Series vii
Foreword ix
Prologue xi
Introduction: Reflexpower™ for
      Willpower Alternative 1
Chapter One: Behold Your Soul's Spirit 15
Chapter Two: Emotional Current 29
Chapter Three: Faculties, Outcome Objectives,
      and Process Goals 41
Chapter Four: Automatic Conflict—Questioning
      Conflict-Provoking Biases and Practicing
      Automatic Mercy 57
Chapter Five: Behavioral Truth Model 69
Chapter Six: Human Reflexes 81
Chapter Seven: Charmingly Disarming—Controlling
      Conflict through Thinking Smart 93
Chapter Eight: Reflexpower for Body Language 103
Chapter Nine: Over the Hump and More—Willpower
      Alternative 115
Epilogue 127
Afterwards 131
Acknowledgments 135
About the Author 137
Bibliography 139

Reflexpower™ Series

It is the author's intention to write a series of books called *Reflexpower™* See a partial list of titles below. As you read this book, think about these other titles and how Reflexpower™ behavioral strategy interfaces with those subjects. I would like to invite you, the reader, to vote on the title that would be of most interest so that we can prioritize the next book. Please go online and cast your vote for the prioritized list of titles that might be of interest to you. Thank you for your continued interest in this new technology that gives you the tools you need to change your mind in a timely fashion and find Reflexpower™ secrets.

Contact us at reflexpowertm@gmail.com.
- *Reflexpower™ for Unifying Rhythms*
- *Reflexpower™ for Mindfulness*
- *Reflexpower™ for Children*
- *Reflexpower™ for Post-Traumatic Growth*
- *Reflexpower™ for Depression Reversal*
- *Reflexpower™ for Peaceful Aging*
- *Reflexpower™ for Happiness*
- *Reflexpower™ for the Meaning of Life*
- *Reflexpower™ for Christians*
- *Reflexpower™ for Nonreligious Humans*
- *Reflexpower™ for Religion*

As an Aside

Reflexpower™ for Addictive Behaviors may be possible but will require the attention of neuroscientists to unravel the relationship of keywords to the addiction. This is an example of the vast potential that may be possible with the discovery of Reflexpower™ technology to change human behavior in a meaningful way, and you, the reader, will find exploring this new frontier exciting.

Foreword

By Richard A. Truax M.D. Psychiatrist

I have known Bill and his wife Shirley over a period of many years. They both have a natural understanding of human behavior and emotions both as it effects themselves and others. Shirley worked on a psychiatric ward with Dr. Lundy a clinical psychologist and myself over a period of years as part of a healing team. She was very effective in that role.

However, this is not a manual on how to treat serious mental illness. It is written for ordinary humans who struggle as most of us do to find meaning, purpose, relevance, peace and love both in our personal life and with others around us. Most of us also seek to be more effective both in our personal and work world. It is for these people that this book is written.

Both Bill and Shirley are committed Christians, however the book mostly avoids theological and psychological language. Bill uses ordinary words. Words that have special meanings such as Reflexpower or willfulness are readily apparent as one reads the book. Dr Lundy in the afterword discusses the book in terms of contemporary psychological theory.

Although a certain caution and humility are in order when discussing other religions than my own; I have spent many hours studying the mystics of Islam, Judaism, Hinduism and Buddhism. It seems they are mostly in agreement that after a period of self discipline and practice there comes a point at which one finds a source of mercy and love that occurs automatically. It appears to come from a higher source that is independent of self-effort. Bill would refer to this as Reflexpower.

However, this does not appear immediately it takes a period of time and consistent practice before it manifests. Likewise Bills approach takes discipline and time. However, it is more streamlined and presented in a way that allows application over a wide variety of beliefs and practices.

Those who have trouble with traditional beliefs may find some modern spiritual writings such as Ken Wilbers Integral Spirituality helpful. Also the findings of quantum physics open the door to a world beyond the exclusively materialistic world of traditional science.

The mindset of a totally materialist world leaves an existential void that contributes to a lack of meaning or purpose as well as despondency and depression for many modern people. Finding a language and method that can open this spiritual world without causing religious arguments and discord would be very helpful. Bills book is an important step in that direction. His key term Reflexpower is not the property of any one religion or belief system.

Prologue

Thirty years ago, I was told a story about a Catholic priest's experience giving parishioners last rites. This story made a lasting impression upon me, and over time, it has given me an insightful understanding of my own soul and how this faculty is pivotal to "living life on life's terms."

In the story with the last rites, there had been a terrible car accident that had taken two family members' lives and left the third member in a coma for more than six weeks. This man had several surgeries, and it appeared he was going to be OK if he recovered from the coma. Complications set in, and he took a rapid turn for the worse. This large family gathered together to be with him in his final hours while the family priest give him his last rites. The Father gave the man his last rites and started praying for God's intervention. Several minutes into the prayer, the man set up in bed fully awake and curtly looked at the priest saying, "Go to hell." He relaxed, closed his eyes, and died.

The family and priest were shocked by the hope of his recovery and devastated by the finality of what he had said. His brief but clear last words would forever be his lasting legacy. They all knew the man was an agnostic believer, but they had no idea of the intensity of his disbelief in the Christian faith. Jesus said in Mark 8:36–37, "For what does it profit a man to gain the whole world, and forfeit his Soul? For what will a man give in exchange for his Soul?"

From this I learn that only those who do not know the soul as a faculty would freely forfeit such a precious part of our being. Depending on a person's philosophical system, a soul can either be mortal or immortal, but nonetheless, the exercise of the soul is the most divine goodness of human action.

We will never know how this recovery transpired, but there are some things we do know: those we surround ourselves with shape and sway our attitudes and lives. This is evidenced by what Gods or people we choose to spend our time with or what privileges we choose. It is generally believed and proved in this story that there are good and evil forces that influence our behavior in profound ways.

So where does internal conflict come from? It is, at least in part, our separation from our soul's principles. What can we learn from this story? We need to spend more time and learn more about our souls. The man who died certainly must have spent a great deal of time with his God to hold such sway over his death, right? We spend more "quality" time with our pets, cell phones, and televisions than many of us do with our soul or the ones we love.

Exercising our soul requires us to have faith in our soul. James W. Fowler (1940–2015) defines faith as an activity of trusting, committing, and relating to the world based on a set of assumptions of how one related to others and the world—thus, living life on life's terms.

Our soul is the very essence of our humanity, which stimulates automatic emotional responses that can quickly change our mind. This book calls that response Reflexpower and aims to help the reader find the commands needed to have willful mercy and a well-directed mind that overcomes conflict with a simple, one-step behavioral strategy. This changes our mind by helping us disarm conflict and amend our attitude. The new technology opens a pathway for us to give voice to our soul, changing our worldview and purpose for life. Exercising our soul is up to us to do with as we see fit. The choice is yours.

To know yourself is to know your soul's heart.

I want to change the world. But I have found that the only thing one can be sure of changing is oneself.
—Aldous Huxley

The unexamined life is not worth living.
—Socrates

Introduction
Reflexpower™ for Willpower Alternative

Mission Statement

Teaching a one-step solution to changing the mind, taking the work out of willpower, putting you at peace with your soul, regardless of religion

In my last position before retiring, I was a Research Fellow for a *Fortune* 500 company. When we worked with outside contract laboratories, we required them to sign a nondisclosure agreement to protect the intellectual property. The problem with these agreements, regardless of how ethical a person someone was, is that when you tell someone new information, you have changed forever how that person will think about the subject. And this is what you, the reader, are about to experience from this book, because it has new information. For example, Malcolm Gladwell's book *Tipping Point* on "how little things can make big difference" changed how we think about the term "tipping point."[1] You will find the many little points that are revealed in Reflexpower will make a big difference because they teach our intuitional memory how to function and what brings us happiness and satisfaction with life. And this is why neuroscientists and people from all walks of life

---

1   Malcolm Gladwell, *Tipping Point* (Boston: Little Brown, 2000).

will find they can get new ideas from the cutting edge of this behavioral-strategies research.

Reflexpower™ for Willpower Alternative is the product of a research project that I started over a decade ago to learn how to disarm conflict without emotional loss so that we can live life on life's terms. One of Thomas Edison's quotes is, "Success is 90% perspiration and 10% inspiration," and that has been the case when unraveling this behavioral challenge. The current world's need for new answers to this old behavioral problem could not be more pressing than it is with the coronavirus pandemic. In the last ninety days, we have worked hard to finalize this book to help everyone cope with living life on life's terms, and by doing this, put color back into life. Let's move on with this interesting new discovery.

The prologue introduces the notion that our soul's will may be separated from our behavioral response, causing us to have internal conflict. And we need to have a well-directed mind that responds to this conflict by connecting our soul with our mind by our brain speaking to our mind in our natural auditory language, thus giving voice to our soul, which is necessary for us to change our minds and attitudes.

> Reflexpower is *smart power*, bringing my verbal and nonverbal worlds together when my mind organizes my *will* and directs my brain to cooperate with my soul, disarming conflict and creating peace.

versus

Willpower is *grunt power* brute force—forcing my *will* upon my soul and other emotions, such as laziness, creating conflict, frustration, anxiety, stress, and anger.

The discovery of Reflexpower's need for redirection establishes a new behavioral understanding of our facilities. Exercising our soul-and-mind brain faculties requires us to communicate in brain language, which we have coined "emotional current." The product of emotional current is automatic reflexes, which we have coined "Reflexpower." Thus, when we give voice to our soul with the proper commands, we stimulate direction. This intriguing story about how I learned to change my attitude can quickly become confusing to the reader, so I will discuss each component in this behavioral strategy separately.

Learning how to *change your mind and attitude* changes the human condition. Like all new technology, if you do not learn to change (in this case, your mind), you will be left behind. Unveiling the secrets of Reflexpower and learning the simple behavioral strategies totally alters life for the better. It is extremely hard to alter our behavior if we do not learn how to channel our responses to stimulate our desired behavior. (Reflexpower is pivotal to change.) This process becomes an automatic system of continuous improvement that unburdens us from emotional angry conflict, stress, anxiety, and frustration.

Our soul's spirit is based upon *willful mercy*, and it becomes the foundational rock our heart builds intuitive love upon. Mercy activates our mind and heart's capacity to love because it alters our behavioral attitude, and it allows us to deepen our relationship to *love*. The principle can best be exemplified by extraordinary morally principled heroes who consciously make the supreme sacrifice of giving up their life for another. This can include a person who jumps into a river to save a drowning child, a soldier who throws his body onto a grenade to save lives of countless people, or a person who runs into a raging fire to save a stranger. We currently are eternally grateful for all for the countless coronavirus health-care workers who selflessly put themselves at risk. This type of conduct demonstrates how sacred mercy's character is to us. The examples above detail extreme mercy, but the truth of the matter is that mercy is attainable in our everyday lives—and usually costs us very little. For example, it can cost nothing to let someone go before you in line or to be considerate of another's feelings, regardless of who they are, or to speed it up when someone is waiting for you in a crosswalk.

Mercy is the beginning of freedom from conflict, or loss (any loss). When sacrifice has a heart and you no longer see sacrifice as a painful ordeal, the soul's virtues are being expressed in willful mercy. This command brings my verbal and nonverbal world together, as it does when I speak to others, and we start to respect and love our neighbors as ourselves.

Willfulness is the universal emotional language that unifies our mercy with another's emotions, causing us to have similar feelings because we are intuitively speaking our soul's language. Mercy is often the most underdeveloped part of our behavior. Lack of *mercy* is an unintended consequence of society's priorities. Mercy is what is glaringly missing from our educational systems at home, at school, and at church because it has become a lost priority. Mercy is a conduit for us to act upon our heart's love, and that makes us feel good about ourselves from the satisfaction we get being merciful. Without loving-kindness, our behavior lacks sincere meaning, and we know this by the empty feeling we have of not being fully human. Bestowing mercy is a welcome relief from the narcissistic arrogant emotions that impedes the joy we get from our soul's goodness.

This lack of mercy in our world is evidenced by the increase in mental health issues that our society is experiencing and elevated suicide rates. Even some of the most successful people who want for nothing have lost this meaningful connection with their soul and resort to a suicidal solution. We all should review how meaningful our soul is to us.

When was the last time you talked to your children about the importance of mercy? Or, for that matter, did your parents ever have this discussion with you? We honor our children by asking them about their food preferences but neglect discussing mercy and then go on to criticize society's lack of compassion. That does not make any sense—but there has not been a book to help us discover the importance of mercy or how to change our mind or behavior, to bring our verbal and nonverbal worlds together, until now.

We are faced with three realities when we selflessly live life on life's terms:

1. We are who we are. Our heart's emotional nature may be selfish.

2. My soul's grace is the unifying source of Reflexpower.

3. Selflessly *living* life on life's terms requires me to acknowledge my soul's mercy and my heart's emotional nature, which can cause me conflict when I do what I do not want to do.

Giving voice to our soul by internally saying, "My soul is merciful" orchestrates disarming Reflexpower when these three realities are faced with conflict. This is the easiest path to changing our mind and heart toward having a willful attitude. This simple one-step behavioral solution stimulates redirection. The joy and satisfaction of being fully human can be achieved "reflexively," by automatically altering our behavioral attitude. This book is devoted to discussing a one-step behavioral solution that changes our mind automatically.

It has never been suggested in the Bible that we will not be subjected to the evil of sin after the Garden of Eden. The original sin from the Garden of Eden is evidenced in our primitive emotional nature to this day. Our hope lies in our soul's merciful goodness, but both good and evil will always be present. Our mind needs to guide our brain with our voice in order to access our soul's goodness. However, by *not* giving voice to the forces of evil, we keep ourselves from sinning. Thus, it is clearly our choices that cause us to sin. Both forces have a powerful draw of their own. The fact that we personally feel these forces means they exist, even though we may not understand their dimensions. This is why some churches talk about mysteries.

Living Life on My Terms: Loss Is Seen as Sacrifice

We have all probably heard the cliché "Don't cry over spilled milk." It has come into use because it makes sense—after the milk is spilled, there is nothing you can do about it. Likewise, the phrase "You cannot unring the bell" suggests that once something is done, it's done. The reason these idioms were established was to point out the obvious, the truth we refuse to acknowledge. This is evidenced when we see loss—any loss we can do nothing about—as a sacrifice. This attitude is one of the main reasons that "living life on my terms" causes us to see loss as sacrifice. This viewpoint only cascades into painful frustration, anxiety, and stress.

We always will be guilty of the need to amend our attitude from time to time because we are human (we are who we are), but now we can face the problem by giving voice to our soul and rejoicing in the goodness of our spirit's presence.

Living Life on Life's Terms: Sacrificial Behavior

When common, everyday sacrifices from conflict are a painful loss to us, that kind of sacrifice depreciates our soul's willfulness. When *sacrifice* is accepted by us with humility, it becomes the high road because sacrifice achieves our goal of being just (unifying mercy), and we are seen by others as the hero. Thus, *sacrificial behavior* makes *mercy* important to us. Often, when we see sacrifice as a painful loss, we are actually taking the amoral low road because we are allowing our primal emotional nature to prevail. The difference between these two pathways has unintended consequences for people who take the low road (read on below). The good news is that when we understand that *intuitive mercy is sacred* as *good news*, it is easy for anyone to alter their behavior. We only have to have a readiness to amend life with truth. However, we cannot amend life without first changing the forgoing attitude about living on *our* terms rather than on *life's* terms.

The language I use sets the tone my brain hears, which orchestrates my nonverbal reflexes. For example, if I am trying to control my conflict with having "spilled milk" and say anything depreciating, like swearing or feeling sorry for myself, it will indeed cascade into painful frustration, anxiety, and stress. This feeling will be present even if I try masking my disappointment by saying, "Whatever" because I only internalized or stuffed my feelings—I have not changed my attitude; my feelings are still only about my loss. However, if I truly live life on life's terms, I would say "In truth-It is what it is," because I have accepted 90 percent of life's disappointment are out of my control, and I am OK with not thinking of only my loss, because my attitude about loss has been altered. The nonverbal, reflexive difference in between saying, "Whatever" and the truth of the fact "In truth-It is what it is," is an affirmative difference.

Living life on life's terms is made easy for those who take the high road because life fortifies their just mercy by rewarding them as heroes, as they should be when they do what is right. What makes living life on life's terms a smart choice is that 90 percent of life's terms cannot be changed by us—after all, we are who we are. However, we can transform our behavioral response. This will be discussed at length later. We should not judge the motives of others' preferences and cannot un-ring the bell. This makes it easy for us to master life's terms with loving-kindness.

Methodology

The operational principle behind this book is the unique claim that people are inherently gifted with their goodness and intelligence. We are born out of a loving goodness that God endowed upon us at birth. In Genesis 1:26, God said, "Let Us make man in Our image, according to Our likeness," hence the origin of our *humanity* being filled with faith, hope, and loving goodness. At the time we were given the spark of life, we were also given our soul's spirit. With today's understanding of genetic makeup, God might say with "our DNA" rather than in "our image." Semantics aside, it is important that we understand how blessed we are to have a soul that is *good.* Our soul's grace, the origin of our humanity, is based upon faith, hope, and loving goodness. Our soul's nature loves willful mercy, and we are born in God's image.

When we experience an internal conflict with our primitive emotional nature that arises from our actions, we are experiencing our willfulness at odds with our emotional nature. We will always experience this internal conflict until we learn to act upon our conscience, interrogate our emotional arrogance, and reroute it with verbal redirection. This behavioral strategy is not meant to alter how you follow Christ; it is meant to help you form a more honest relationship with yourself. Aside from the accepted truths in the Bible, we all differ on how we view our faith, and the diversity of that fact creates a rich and wonderful global faith community. What is more, learning how to nurture and pull ourselves closer in line with our intent is universal. Learning to use Reflexpower to align oneself with one's inner mercy is an act of love that is not limited but instead strengthened and bolstered by our diversity and individuality.

Reflexpower posits a behavioral strategy that will give you the tools you need to live an effortlessly selfless life. Most people realize the virtues of being selfless and would prefer to live in true harmony with others. The only dilemma that presents itself here is *how* to achieve this true harmonic state—namely, how to let our loving-kindness prevail over our conceit and learned self-importance. This book tackles the puzzle of opposing thoughts that our mind is susceptible to in an effort to teach thoughtful, merciful behavior and to eliminate thoughtless hypocrisy.

It is only through the rewiring and rerouting of our Reflexpower that we can teach transparent truth to our emotional nature. Reflexes are often thought of as automatic behaviors, or how the brain initiates a certain action based on a learned impulse. This book aims to teach you how to want to love others and how this impulse stems from selflessly acting upon mercy's impulses until they become reflexes, or automatic behaviors. We will disarm the everyday fallacies that we live with, the inner conflicts that we ignore, and the behavior we deny—all by learning how to master control over our mind and emotional nature in order to act upon our true and virtuous character with loving-kindness.

The presence of love, peace, and harmony cannot be achieved until we learn to willfully cooperate because *cooperation* unifies our faculties, creating love.

The Need for *Mercy*

The recent goals of many mindfulness and emotional intelligence theories have centered on the idea of identifying the forces that create conflict between the specifics of our heart's emotional nature and our principles. Here, in *Reflexpower*, our object is to redirect the conflict that arises from these opposing influences. This way, we are not doing away with reasoning or feelings; rather, we are finding *a solution* to the conflict that arises when we are misguided into arrogant behavior. The one-step solution is simply to reroute conflict with reflexes of our choice. This way, a chain of command forms outside of our default behaviors and patterns, allowing us to live freely and in harmony by giving internal voice to our soul.

As an Aside

As the author, my biases are Christian, but my quoted Christian examples have no influence on the behavioral mechanics of this behavioral model. Inviting the reader to effectively use all faculties that your brain deals with (reflexes, emotional nature, and soul) is the genesis of the behavioral model. Because of our biases on such foundational subjects (religion and lifestyle), the reader is sure to have well-developed ideas that are not relevant to this behavioral model and can cause functional fixedness, which is not the reader's fault. Reflexpower is truly new material about very old subject matter, which warrants unfreezing your brain with new thinking.

The reader does not have to do anything to change his or her behavior other than to give his or her soul a voice in order to change the mind and become fully human. This behavioral model does not require the burden of self-control willpower—it transforms us from within when we use all our faculties to avoid stress, anxiety, and frustration that can lead to displeasure or even anger. Thus, be *merciful* to yourself and those you care about.

Final Word

The reader of this book need not have a background in psychology to follow the *principled* point of my story or the lesson. Reflexpower has been written in a narrative format in order to provide the most accessible of experiences to readers from all walks of life. The tenets of my behavioral strategy are reduced down to simple principles and explained through experience and example. My goal in this format is to allow you, the reader, to experience this story and learn from the observation of my behavior because it is often easier to observe and learn from others than to put the onus of such a change on oneself. As you read this book, observe your engagement with mercy's reflexes; in this way, you can easily apply the message of this book to your own life and live a happier and more humanistic one that gives you satisfaction. We can be good people, and I know you feel that this subject is important—otherwise, you would not be reading this introduction. Now is the time to act upon your readiness to amend your life and your behavior with those you love and care about.

Chapter One
Behold Your Soul's Spirit

No other creatures on earth but humans have souls that make them aware of faith, hope, and love principles. This is what makes the human experience unique. Unfortunately, in our society, we give little thought to our soul, with or without religion, leaving us with an unbalanced behavioral pattern and at a loss of how to include our principles in our behavior. Reflexpower aims to shed a new light on this interesting subject in addition to the obvious religious aspects.

How do I make my soul a priority? By being at peace with my soul so that I can change my attitude about the most influential faculty in the body. Any sincere behavioral change starts by amending our attitude, and we all know this is true. We will be talking more about amending our attitude later in this chapter.

The protagonist in Reflexpower is our soul's spirit. This is a good time to introduce our protagonist because it is the solution to many of our behavioral conditions. Our indwelling soul is the self's conscience, which we *trust* to tell us what is right from wrong. Our soul is the *heart* and conscience of faith, hope, and love. We are born in God's image, with a soul full of merciful goodness that is a gift, one that is available to all of mankind, to be used as we see fit.

What we may not have given enough credit for is our soul's *hope* for us, which is *peace*, and it only wants what is best for us. Hence our soul wants the proclivity of our emotional nature to see others and the world as it sees us—full of hope that sees the good in us, others, and the world so that we may be at peace. The proclivity of our hope dramatically changes how our emotional nature functions because it establishes a foundation for peace when we are hopeful. Hope's peace is dynamic, not needing to be judged when we see that which is good and endless possibilities. Hope that is based upon truth frees our emotional self's loss because we are no longer tied to the self's ego or biases.

I'd like to spend some time talking about our emotional nature and soul. Our primitive emotional response can be self-centered, and that causes us to be judgmental. Our soul's spirit is the exact opposite—selfless, merciful, and nonjudgmental—causing us no internal conflict. The origin of our goodness is the faith we have in hope and love that speaks to our conscience about "what is the right thing to do," and that can cause conflict when our emotional behavior is not balanced with our soul's intuitive mercy.

The beauty of this gift is that the power of our goodness won't be taken away from us if we secularly misuse the gift—in most cases. Jesus said this about God: "for He causes His sun to rise on *the* evil and *the* good, and sends rain on *the* righteous and *the* unrighteous" (Matt. 5:45). We do not have to establish our goodness; we are born with goodness. This goodness is expressed by us when we have sincere love and treat others mercifully. How we mold this gift is another story that is entirely up to us.

We should consider the totality of God's grace, as noted above in Matthew. God's grace is extended to the righteous and the unrighteous, which sets an unrestricted, selfless example for us to follow. In reality, because this requires us to experience the loss of our emotional arrogance in totality, we cannot follow God's example by ourselves. My emotional nature can be self-centered by nature, and I need the grace of my indwelling soul to sacrifice such a loss. By acknowledging my loss verbally, I give voice to mercy, fearing my emotional nature. This unifying statement gives my mind the strength to accept my loss and rejoice in the goodness of my spirit. This is what makes me fully human. We experience this condition every time we experience doing what is right and what is not in our best interest. We make the most informed choices when we use all our faculties (verbal and nonverbal), unifying our mind, emotional nature, and soul. Love cannot flourish with two masters.

Here is a short illustration of giving one's soul a voice while living life on life's terms. Let's imagine finding $10,000 in a brown paper bag that someone legitimately lost. Upon finding the money and discovering the amount of money, I quickly say, "Have mercy" (with a willful attitude), as I know I need to find who the legitimate owner is, thus doing what is right. My emotional nature might have larcenous emotions about the money. However, by quickly giving my conscience a voice, allowing me to change my mind, the results of my behavior have been greatly improved to do the right thing without entertaining bad behavior. This demonstrates how we can influence our feeling of loss and improves our behavior with peace and how we feel about the world. This method can help me to change how I feel about finding $10,000, letting someone in line ahead of me, or alleviating the displeasure of being grievously wronged.

Why define the soul as merciful or as having loving-kindness? It is intuitively at peace, seeing the best in us and the world. Our soul is the heart of our love, and the one word that defines love's authenticity is *mercy*. When Jesus was discussing with his disciples their relation to each other in John 15:12–13, he commanded them to love one another and said, "Greater love has no one than this, that one lay down his life for his friends." Hence, the notion of *mercy* defines our soul and authentic loving-kindness.

The word *love* in our everyday vernacular is used to describe everything, from basic things ("I love the color blue") to highly complex emotions ("I am devoted to loving my wife or husband"). But we also can abuse the word *love* by using it in insincere ways. People all over the world and throughout history have grappled with the meaning of love, and countless pieces of literature have struggled to define it. For example, C. S. Lewis's book *The Four Loves* tries to define what love means by categorizing love into four distinct areas. But at the end of the day, the truth of this matter is this: *love is not an emotion.* We think of love as our highest emotion, and love has been commercialized by our society as a highly desirable emotion, but that is a misunderstanding of the true nature of emotion. Emotions are indeed faculties that process information. However, emotions are only capable of strong feelings because emotions were one of the first faculties we had in our evolutionary history. And emotions are some of the most complex and fastest-acting faculties we have. Thus, the conservative definition of an emotion is a facial expression or an affective representation of a basic reaction, such as a reflex from emotional current. Love, by contrast, is an outcome objective that our faculties build via process goals using forces such as willfulness and mercy. We will be talking more about outcome objectives and process goals in the third chapter.

What is emotional current? Emotions are strong feelings. We have coined those feelings to be *current* so that we do not become entangled in the complexity of emotions. At this point in time, there is no scientific consensus on a definition.

If love is not an emotion and is, as I have suggested, an outcome objective, then what is love? I want you, the reader, to *stop* for a moment and answer the above question to your complete satisfaction. As stated in the above paragraph, "People all over the world and throughout history have grappled with the meaning of love, and countless pieces of literature have struggled to define it"—so what is your definition of *love*? This is not a trick question; I am going to give you what I have found about love in the third chapter, but it would be more meaningful to you if you came up with the answer on your own.

There is no mistaking what is meant about love to your mind and heart or to others when you say, "Have mercy," and that is why merciful love is a loving quality we would all love to receive. The words *willfulness* and *mercy* are keywords that makes it possible to design a simple one-step behavioral solution, which stimulates a behavioral change that seriously strengthens the character of our loving-kindness and the satisfaction we get from love. Amending our behavioral objectives alters our attitude, making it easy for us to transform our selfish free will because the stimulation is an automatic, reflexive response that we will be talking more about. By giving my heart's emotion a positive voiced recognition, this communicates my willingness to follow my soul's grace. When I speak with one infused voice command, that brings my verbal and nonverbal worlds together; it transforms my behavioral attitude, allowing me to change my mind.

Understanding the need for keyword voice commands to switch our behavior gives us the tools we need to act upon what is sacred to us, such as peace, loving-kindness, and doing what is right. Through the isolation of one single faculty, Reflexpower, from emotional current or other nonverbal reactions, we are rewiring and subliminally communicating with the mind, using its own language and sharing our life with our soul. Reflexpower can also be used to redirect emotional current conflict by verbalizing a word or phrase that has a known preverbal reflexive response. Here are examples.

1. If you call a person stupid, the "emotional current" of the word *stupid* would stimulate *negative* Reflexpower, which would deliver "automatic willpower." You wanted to insult the person.

2. If you call a person smart, the "emotional current" of the word *smart* would stimulate *positive* Reflex-

power, which would deliver "automatic willpower." You wanted to compliment the person.

3. If you are in conflict with a person and wanted to control your biases or ego and tell yourself to *have mercy*, "emotional current" would stimulate disarming passive Reflexpower, which would deliver "automatic willpower."

4. If you are having internal conflict with your soul's conscience and are conflicted and tell yourself to *be willful*, "emotional current" would disarm the conflict with Reflexpower, which would deliver "automatic willpower."

Thus, a well-directed mind can be in control of their behavior without the use of self-controlled willpower.

We have long been aware of fight-or-flight reflex responses but not of how to control the reflex. In this way, it is easier to act upon our true intentions, committed love, and cooperation, and not default into mindless arrogance.

Reflexpower Commands

What we call this *involuntary automatic reflex faculty response* is Reflexpower, because it accomplishes self-control commands without the need for willpower. It is a superior faculty to willpower because it requires no effort, once Reflexpower becomes a learned, functional, fixed reflex. The problem with self-control commands that require willpower is that most of our bad habits are due to laziness or lack of willpower. This basic flaw in our character is mastered with Reflexpower commands because they are automatically irresistible.

Secret Reflexpower: Disable the Mind When Off, and Enable the Mind When On

When I ignore my soul and do not voice my will to cooperate, I give my emotional arrogance permission to do what I do not want to do. And what I have faith in but do not give Reflexpower to, I will not act upon. My heart is in my soul, doing what I want done. When my mind speaks to my emotional nature for me to willfully cooperate, I do what I want done because my heart's emotion directs my emotional reflexive current. My mind, emotional current, and soul are now acting in harmony.

The secret to Reflexpower is our infused voice command that changes our mind, behavior, and attitude. By *not* using these commands, we disable our mind, regardless of which facility or emotion is involved. This is not our fault because we were not aware of the secret Reflexpower ability to disable or enable our mind.

Recently, I had an experience that illustrates how hidden information about an often-used switch can be amazingly helpful. I have a pickup that I have had for years and loan out from time to time to friends. The pickup is equipped with an automatic headlamp system that uses the headlights as running lights in the daytime when the light switch is in the proper position. Sometimes when the pickup is returned, the daytime running lights are disabled, and I am always frustrated because I do not know how to reactivate the system because the light switch had been in the proper position. It was always necessary for me to manually turn on the lights because a warning buzzer was activated to warn the driver the headlights were off. However, the lights always reactivated themselves after I used the pickup, but I never understood why. One person recently borrowed the pickup three times in one week, disabling the headlights each time, prompting me to go to the instruction manual to figure out the problem ("When all else fails, read the manual").

My driveway is on a hill. When I park the pickup in the driveway, I back into it until the back wheels are in contact with a curb at the end of the driveway, not requiring me to set the parking break. This person always set the brake, which is a good habit. However, setting the break disables the daytime running lights so that you can idle the truck without running the headlights. Problem solved after all these years of frustration. This is an excellent example of the need to know how our mind works.

What keeps us from successfully dismissing our emotional ego or biases to overcome conflict? It is the exceptions that we make. Exceptions destroy the rules and internal guides we know we should follow. Our life's purpose is continuous improvement so that we can become more fully human. In order to do this, we must allow our soul to transform us and challenge us for the better. It is what we do often that changes our mind and attitude. If we fill our lives with exceptions, the *virtuous rules of life never mature us.* Never let the exceptions keep you from doing what you know in your heart you were meant to do.

It is true that exceptions destroy rules, but the bigger problem is the lack of rules to direct our minds when it comes to dealing with our souls. With the absence of rules, a void or vacuum has been established and filled by our emotional ego or biases that displace our influence upon our behavior. By neglecting to give voice to our soul, it is "out of sight, out of mind."

Two Basic Rules

Listed below are two basic rules about our "heart, soul, and mind" faculties that the book's author encourages readers to follow:

1. The first, most important rule: My mind needs to give my soul a voice if I am to share my life with my soul and benefit from its willful spirit, which seeks what is best and sees the good in me. This gives me a needed pathway to shed my ego because the spirit is principled, and I trust my conscience to do what is right. As my emotional nature becomes associated with my soul, I remove my ego.

2. The second rule: My mind needs to tell my brain to use words that stimulate positive *emotional current*, giving my soul a voice that can be heard by my heart to redirect my emotional nature, giving my soul recognition by verbally voicing or chanting:

- *Willful mercy*: "My soul is willfully merciful." Thus, be willful, or have mercy.

By giving my soul a universal voice when I have conflicting or opposing thoughts and negative emotions, and by stimulating my mind to verbally confirm my will by saying, "Be willful" or "Have mercy," I disassociate my emotional arrogance for selflessness. For example, when I say to my mind, "Be willful," it changes my mind's attitude with *emotional current* to be willful, and my mind has become connected to my soul. The problem that arises if I do not disarm my emotional arrogance with a verbal command is that I will remain unable to change.

These key words or phrases give the soul voice so that my heart's *emotional current* and soul's grace become one. My soul's *emotional current* brings another dimension to my humanity because it is intuitively selfless. *My definition of being "fully human" is bringing our verbal and awakened nonverbal worlds together.* When our brain accepts the "soul's principles," it is in concert with the mind's direction, making it irresistible to refuse to do what is right—hence, having unshakable faith in nonverbal Reflexpower. This is why key words are so powerful and must be carefully crafted so that we do what we want done automatically. We will be examining how and why we need to carefully speak to different faculties throughout the book. Later, we will be looking at other behavioral conditions that use "willfulness" or "mercy" as key phrases to direct reflexes so that I can do what I want to do. And there will be a chapter on reflexes. I also will be talking more about sharing life with our soul in the following behavioral model and throughout the balance of the book.

Our soul's hope and peace are not denied to me or any human being. However, we have the power to deny ourselves the benefit of the soul's presence by not communicating with it. What we have not realized is that our mind is obligated to verbally speak to our faculties if we are to overcome behavioral conflict by not using all our faculties. For example, the more I call upon my soul to direct the heart, the more willfully selfless I become. The more I associate with my soul, the more peaceful joy I receive from changing my attitude to a willful attitude. Not having a willful attitude is like attending a feast without an appetite—it cancels the meaningful joy of the feast. It costs me nothing to be *willfully at peace* with others and self after I *willfully detach myself from my judgmental emotional self.* Loss no longer has meaning.

Sharing my life with my soul transforms my behavioral center of gravity for the better. Your soul's advice is sacred and is the most productive advice available to you because it speaks the truth for your inner conscience to do what is right for you. And the best thing that comes from this relationship is the realization that *I am never alone.*

At the close of each chapter, I have composed a question about a theme of the chapter to help you, the reader, interrogate your emotional arrogance, which is usually detrimental and fosters a negative-minded culture, suppressing your mind's confidence to be willful. Take time to reflect upon your inner intelligence. Acknowledge your willful soul, not your emotional arrogance, which may not be your fault. The proclivity of your emotions may be arrogant because of your natural character or for many other reasons. Now that you have been introduced to the benefits of Reflexpower behavioral solutions, you are responsible for any selfishness that inhibits the goodness of your soul.

Acknowledge your willful soul, not your emotional arrogance. Is your heart's emotional nature humble enough to share life with your soul's willful nature?

Notes

Chapter Two

Emotional Current

You Are What You Perceive

A few years ago, I went to the audiologist to be fitted for a hearing aid. The process required testing the equipment's effect on my ability to hear with the hope that, after some tuning, we would find a frequency that worked to better my auditory perception. What should have been a routine procedure became frustrating for me because the hearing aid exacerbated my preexisting condition of tinnitus. Now, I've had tinnitus—a continued ringing in the ears—for some thirty-five years, and I had learned to cope with it. However, when the audiologist tuned the hearing aid, the ringing became amplified and canceled much of the hearing aid benefit. When I told her what the problem was, she told me something so simple yet something so truthful that it changed my entire reality: "You only perceive the ringing."

It was true. In my three-plus decades of dealing with this condition, I had never thought about it this way. It turns out that sometimes until you are forced to describe a situation or think about a condition in a more distanced way, you never have the opportunity to realize how intangible it is. This is also true of emotions such as mercy; we perceive them individually, and they are only real to our mind and not anybody else's. How's that as food for thought?

Hold On, Hold On! One at a Time

Have you heard of the term "hangry"? If you have not, let me explain its origin. Recent pop science and pop culture writers have coined this portmanteau in order to describe the feeling of being so hungry that one turns angry. Thus, those experiencing "hangry-ness" are said to be feeling the mixed emotion of being both hungry and angry at the same time.

For example, someone experiencing a particularly long wait time at a restaurant might say to their friends, "We've been waiting for our food for almost forty-five minutes! This is so ridiculous. I'm getting hangry." Popular terms such as this one perpetuate the idea of *mixed emotions*, or having the ability to sustain more than one emotion at the same time. While it is true that hunger can cause grumpiness and that these feelings of hunger and anger can cycle, these two feelings can never coexist.

Humans can experience a base of six emotions: anger, disgust, fear, happiness, sadness, and surprise. Each emotion can only be experienced on its own, not while paired with another. The term *mixed emotions* has evolved in order to describe the rapid pace with which humans can cycle through these experiences or through a series of emotions, but it has mistakenly come to imply that it is possible to feel two things at once. While it is true that I can feel happy for a moment and then I can feel sad for a moment, I cannot experience happiness and sadness at the same time.

Using the fMRI (functional magnetic resonance imaging) machine, scientists are now able to see how the brain responds and processes emotions in real time, and it has proven that it is, in fact, impossible for us to feel two emotions at the same time. The psychiatric community is very interested in this phenomenon and in the science behind it. The better we understand the way our brain filters emotions and reflexes, the better we can serve others and ourselves. Because we have proven that the brain can only experience one feeling at a time, I posit that we therefore can choose our emotions and also control them. When we describe having "mixed feelings," what we are really doing is indicating that our mind has opposing views on the topic at hand, views that contradict one another and thus cause tension.

So now that we know that the brain can only experience a singular emotion at one time, what can we do with this knowledge to be more selfless or to put this information into good practice? For starters, we can acknowledge that each perceived emotion is merely information to be processed.

Informational Emotion: The Intangibility of Feelings

Many of us attach a great deal of importance to emotions. The way we react to the world around us can shape our experience of life. But the truth is, our primitive emotions are not capable of executive reasoning and are merely perceptions from the emotional current generated by the situation, and those perceptions from *emotional current* are able to convey pieces of information to be fed to the brain. If we treat our perceptions or emotions as though they exist independently of the brain, as though they are tangible, or have any grounds in reality, we create a world in which we are chaining ourselves and others to an imagined and unpredictable standard. Moreover, when we react to situations emotionally, we create a reality based on a perception and illusion.

Reaching back to an experience I had with tinnitus would make a good example to illustrate how important it is to accept life on life's terms, even when it is a perception and/or illusion. My audiologist suggested I join a class led by a psychologist to help veterans deal with the effects of tinnitus on everyday living. The first thing they did during the class was going around the table and having each member introduce himself or herself and describe how tinnitus impacted his or her life. As each person described his or her problems, there was a commonality in the problematic issues: the interruption of sleep. About 75 percent of the class had tinnitus less than five years, and about 25 percent of the class, like me, had experienced tinnitus for decades. I was shocked that sleep was a problem for people who had long-term tinnitus. I had overcome the problem with sleep and most, if not all, the other problems that were revealed. Hearing about the problems brought back memories of my issues with them as well. But I quickly realized that the reason I no longer experienced these issues was that, after my initial diagnosis, I accepted the fact the *information* was not going to change and I would have to learn to live with the noise as it got progressively worse over time. My problem is that the noise from tinnitus can become so loud, it interferes with understanding what is being said. At this point in time, there is no solution for that problem.

In order to break out of this system, it is important to think about our emotional perceptions as information that is distributed throughout our body with emotional current. The brain, after all, can reason with information, but it cannot reason with *emotional current.* When we realize how intangible emotions are, we are able to rename emotional feelings as *emotional current information* and practice rerouting our responses via new understanding and pathways.

Emotional Current Informational Pathway

So how do we turn feelings into information and reroute them via a new pathway? It's easy. The first step in creating a pathway for emotional current information is to *consider your options* and ask yourself, "What is my plan?" Having a plan is always a safety net in reminding yourself about what is at stake and what your primary directive is. If you have no plan, there will be no progress. Once you have reminded yourself that your primary directive—your plan—is to use the behavioral model in order to reroute reflexes. The next step is to deliberate emotional current information with executive reasoning, remembering that your emotions are just informational current. Emotional current stimulates feelings that give us another dimension to information. Thus, information is not complete until the mind deliberates how we feel about the information. And those feelings can be amended with Reflexpower. Negative or emotional arrogance triggers negative reflexes; likewise, merciful, cooperative emotions trigger willful reflexes. Reminding yourself to "be merciful," because your behavioral objective is cooperation, prompts you to give voice to your soul's grace. These verbal redirections then send the emotional current signal to the brain that willful cooperation is the key to unification, to which the mind responds accordingly. Thus, I accept the loss of my emotional arrogance for the peace and joy of selflessness.

For example, if I tell myself *not* to get irritated when someone is rude to me, this activity will have little effect upon my mind because I have already personalized the irritation through creating a relationship between the problem and myself. Even though I am telling myself not to get irritated, my mind is telling my brain that it should be through the implication that there is something to be mad about. However, when conflict arises, I can chose to cooperate with the emotion by saying, "Have mercy," or "I'm good with that," or "What can I learn from this so it will not happen again?" These verbal redirections give voice to my soul's grace when I have released myself from internal emotional current. The conflict is no longer personal to me. You can have only one emotion at a time, and when it cooperates with your soul's goodness, the self is solidly in control.

Emotional Current and You

We have spent a great deal of time talking about how to react when an activity or someone's behavior causes an undesirable emotional reaction. However, we have spent little time thinking about ourselves and how our behavior can also provoke unwanted emotional reactions in others. While it's admirable to try to be selfless and kind all of the time, it's also improbable that we will fulfill this task all of our waking moments. Often a moment of irritation can result in saying something mean, cruel, painful, or unjust to someone we love or care about. We can later redact this emotional response by saying we "misspoke." While this may sound like a Band-Aid meant to cover up dirty and truthful feelings, the fact of the matter is, we do misspeak as humans, and we say things that are hurtful and regrettable. And these conflicts usually arise out of our perceptions and emotional responses. However, the best way to combat these situations, even while they are occurring, is to remember that the final thing we say (to ourselves or to others) triggers the final outcome and dictates our emotional current response: we *are* what we *do* and *say*, so we should try to keep it merciful. "Be willful," and remember emotional feelings are just emotional current information.

In order to combat the permanent damage to our goal and bring ourselves back toward the path of selflessness, it's important to always end on a good note, even when conflict has started. You can diffuse the situation by saying, "I'm sorry I misspoke because I was feeling upset" or "I love you, and you know that. What I just said is not true. I am just upset about the situation and reacted thoughtlessly." By ending on a cooperative final thought or verbal utterance, we are not only reinforcing our behavioral strategy and our desired temperament, but we are also preventing further damage to our relationship with others by defusing the emotional temperature of the situation. Reconciliation with others requires disarming the emotional response, which is something we have influence and control over. This is another example of the disarming benefit, and it allows us to change our mind and attitude in the same fashion in which it defuses conflict. Reconciliation gives voice to our spirit, unifying our emotional current with others.

Emotional Current: A Long-Term Outlook

It's easy to think about the short-term application of emotional current, but how can we look toward reinforcing and creating a long-term plan for our cooperation via emotional responses? One easy way in which we can do this is to journal, keeping a living archive of our emotional responses and triggers. Once I started logging things that made me upset or events that seemed to act as my emotional triggers, I began to notice a pattern and reminded myself that most of these situations were out of my control, and even more so, that after some time had passed, many—if not most—of the situations were not really that upsetting after I had time to think about them. Once I started using the behavioral model and plan, cooperation became more of a primary directive for me, and soon enough, my journal entries became more and more sparse.

For example, one entry contained my annoyance about having to wait almost fifteen minutes to be served my coffee at a restaurant. As I logged my emotional response and practiced the behavioral model, I came to the cooperative conclusion of "They are doing their best." And suddenly, the conflict was defused, and my emotional response was rerouted via a cooperative pathway. And you know what? Eventually my coffee arrived, and it tasted just as good as it would have had it arrived five minutes earlier. My biases, which I thought were nonnegotiable, were rewritten just like that, and a unifying new peaceful experience took place in the mind. Finding the good in others and situations is in lockstep with keeping peace with all concerned.

Another way to reinforce this strategy is to take a long-term outlook on emotional current information and spend more time thinking and appreciating the joy of life. If you are anything like me and like most of humanity, you can sometimes find yourself spending countless hours and minutes "thinking" back, revisiting, and lamenting over negative or resentful encounters, stewing like a slow-cooking Crock-Pot. Just as you become angrier and more upset when you dwell on a negative experience, the inverse is also true: the more you spend time thinking about the positive aspects of a situation or a person, the happier you become to know them, or the more eager you become to find a positive, selfless direction out of conflict.

When we think of ourselves as lucky, we internalize the credit for positive things that happen to us. By doing this, we miss a grand opportunity to assign credit to the faculties that actually caused the good fortune. By rerouting how we handle the positive that happens to us, we strengthen this behavioral model and our lease on life. We start thinking of ourselves as being blessed rather than being lucky because we are living life on life's terms by being fully human and not selfishly narcissistic, which is often not our fault; we did not consider our nonverbal soul. Thus, when we change, we become grateful, and that positive emotional current comes from the presence of our soul.

As a wrap-up, let's go over a partial list of the beneficial aspects of emotional current and review the richness that information can bring into your life and your mission.

The Benefits of Emotional Current

- Peace-loving emotional current gives us the strength to live life on life's terms, freeing us of judging others' motives.
- Unifying our soul's merciful peace with our heart's emotional current encourages us to be grateful, dwelling on our goodness, rewriting our temperament.
- When emotions are rewritten in our mind as nonverbal information, we can deliberate with that emotional information and verbally control our response.

Acknowledge your willful soul, not your emotional arrogance. Does your soul's grace transform your heart's emotional nature and mind's grateful attitude?

Notes

Chapter Three

Faculties, Outcome Objectives, and Process Goals

Reflexpower behavioral strategy uses the product of the mind's faculties to achieve your principled outcome objectives and process goals. This brief background information helps you understand how the faculties work together to stimulate *Reflexpower™ for Willpower Alternative* and the strategies used to have a well-directed mind.

FACULTIES: HEART, SOUL AND MIND
Heart

Our mind's heart is a primitive (nonverbal) faculty that man has always possessed, and it communicates with the body and brain through emotional current. The heart does not have deliberating capabilities or process information as the mind. The heart communicates nonverbal information to others through facial expressions, body language, voice tone, et cetera, and to the brain and body with emotional current. Our heart is the epicenter of emotions, and they can be redirected with keywords or phrases that develop emotional current. We know from fMRI results that when emotions are stimulated by key words, the brain uses the basic section of the brain called the basal ganglia, which communicates emotional facial expressions and the like through the limbic system. The mind's heart does not deliberate information; it only uses basic, low-level reasoning that is communicated with emotional current to the brain, mind, and body.

This new understanding of Reflexpower puts us on notice that we cannot trust heartfelt emotions to be principled, unless the emotion is influenced by the soul's willful principles that the mind has communicated to the brain's auditory voice. Heartfelt emotions stimulate emotional current, which gives us our behavior feeling from the six basic emotions: anger, disgust, fear, happiness, sadness, and surprise, discussed in the last chapter. Thus, emotions can be principled or can *originate from any of the seven deadly sins*. Our brain accumulates emotional information for our mind to direct the heart and include the soul, being responsible for having well-directed faculties. This new information will help the mind to be less *naive* about heartfelt emotions and points out the great need for this behavioral-strategy methodology to control conflict from these three faculties (heart, soul, and mind). We will talk more about this as we get into directing our faculties.

Soul

Like the heart, our soul is a primitive nonverbal faculty that communicates to the body via our conscience. Our soul is a principled faculty that filters our heart's emotions through our mind's executive reasoning, telling us right from wrong. The soul is like our heart—it also uses emotional current that can be redirected with key words or phrases that develop emotional current to communicate nonverbal information or direct information internally. The soul's basic reasoning is a "low-level principled reasoning"; thus, it does not deliberate its decisions. This function, again, is reserved for the mind.

Mind

The mind is the set of cognitive faculties, including consciousness, imagination, perception, thinking, judgment, language, and memory, which is housed in the brain. Our mind is the only set of faculties that processes information with executive reasoning. From fMRI machines, we have been given an insight into when the mind is using executive reasoning. The mind is obligated to call upon the brain to give voice to our soul's conscience or any other *preferred instruction* from emotional current when the mind finds it appropriate. Why is the brain obligated to give voice to the soul? That is a great question. In order to change your mind, your brain has to speak to your mind's faculties in our natural auditory language, and that command to the brain comes from our mind's complex cognation of the *self's* will. You cannot become master of your domain until you can control your Reflexpower redirection by having a well-directed mind.

Neuroscientists have long accepted that our ability to change our mind or behavior is controlled via a single region within the brain's prefrontal cortex, an area involved in planning and other high mental functions. It has been recently found that last-minute decision-making is a lot more complicated than previously known. Our mind's set of faculties is what allows us to have subjective awareness, which includes the central nervous system, emotional current, and nonverbal activities. What the brain does not verbalize to the mind, we will not have subjective awareness of, and that is what causes us to do what we do not want to do, and *we will not change*. Thus, for the brain to change its mind and be in control of its Reflexpower, the mind's brain voice faculty is obligated to speak for the soul's conscience and other nonverbal information.

What has not been unraveled is the use of Reflexpower. The one universal language that the heart, soul, and mind uses is nonverbal Reflexpower from emotional current or other nonverbal information. Reflexpower is a simple behavior in mechanistic terms and does not require complex cognation. This is the *new universal language strategy* we have developed for this behavioral model to disarm conflict without emotional loss, communicate willful cooperation, and transform our attitude. Reflexpower is not even on neuroscientists' or psychiatrists' radar screens, which is evidenced by the fact that our definition of Reflexpower has not been published and is not in the dictionary.

This explanation of the mind explains the statement made in the introduction: "Learning how to *change your mind* changes the human condition. Like all new technology, if you do not learn to change (in this case, your mind), you will be left behind." We will be discussing these interesting faculties throughout the book.

Outcome Objectives: Faith, Hope, and Love—Process Goals

Faith, hope, and love are the foundational outcome objectives of our process goals, and they transform us because they can change our mind and attitude with "willfulness" and "mercy."

- Faith: The verbal expression of our mind that stimulates emotional current

- Hope: A nonverbal proclivity of our mind that stimulates negative or positive attitude

- Love: A awakened nonverbal expression of our heart's emotional current

This book is built upon the mind using verbal faculties to direct (or redirect) emotional current that stimulates nonverbal Reflexpower. Our behavior changes by having productive outcome objectives and process goals. For example, when I see *love* as a commitment, my process goal is to be attached. This demonstrates how important it is to understand the outcome objective.

In the Bible, Saint Paul said, "And now these three remain: faith, hope and love. But the greatest of these is love" (1 Cor. 13:13). Faith, hope, and love are outcome objectives that bring color to our behavior in an otherwise black-and-white, right-or-wrong perception of life. Faith is the verbal expression of our mind and thus the voiced interpretation of how the mind feels about our behavior, and how the mind feels about nonverbal hope, nonverbal love, and the mind's faith in all other nonverbal activity. As stated earlier, Reflexpower brings my verbal and awakened nonverbal worlds together; therefore, it can also bring clarity to my faith. Plus, bringing my verbal and nonverbal worlds together is what makes me fully human, and that can bring order and color to my objectives. This explanation is not meant to confuse you; it explains the working inner connection and sway of faith, hope, and love from most perspectives. Reflexpower is an inclusive behavioral solution, and that is the reason it is so effective in disarming most conflict. Many other solutions only affect part of the problem and can be difficult to use.

It is actually not our fault that many of us do not experience continuous improvement in honing our faith to disarm conflict so that we amend our behavior to mirror our principles. As I stated above, "Faith is the verbal expression of our mind that stimulates emotional current," and that is the same simple behavior mechanism as nonverbal Reflexpower methodology for amending our behavior. The difference is that our mind is responsible for giving the voice command to stimulate emotional current that calls upon our Reflexpower. This strategy has not been considered before; therefore, it is not our fault that we find it difficult to follow our faith. For example, if my faith does not call upon my soul to "be willful" or "have mercy," it is up to me to do what is right by giving a voice command to stimulate emotional current that calls upon my Reflexpower. In this way, I can support my faith when conflict arises to achieve continuous improvement. You will see how this works as we make our way through the balance of the book.

Love

In the first chapter, I asked you to define what love meant to you, and then I promised that I would share my thoughts with you. For me, my understanding of love is as follows:

- *Commitment* to love is the one principle that describes the meaning of love.

- *Attachment* to the one you love is a process goal that fulfils your commitment.

Satisfying, long-lasting love comes from peaceful attachment; thus, love is my deepest expression of gratitude, which is a sustainable love.

When commitment to love is no longer a sacrifice, you are in love.

For me, the word *love* is reserved for those to whom I am attached, or those to whom I want to commit. I had to know that *commitment* is love's outcome objective if I am to have a productive process goal like *attachment*, to find satisfaction with love. This is why I asked you to define what love means to you. The choices are yours to make.

Summary of Love

Love is probably the most unsuccessful human endeavor we are faced with in life. Look at the dismal divorce rate, and observe married couples' satisfaction with love or, for that matter, the level of happiness within our society. We have continued conflict with other nations, causing wars and rumor of wars. Our faith-based endeavors that are based upon *love* have no more success with true love—"the kind of love that the blind can see and the deaf can hear"—than the general population. Why is this? Why have we bothered to go to the moon when we do not personally solve this basic foundational behavioral need for love? The reasons are many, and truly, new solutions are few, but perhaps the greatest problem is we do not truthfully interrogate our behavioral principles or faith.

The principles that have been suggested with *Reflexpower™ for Willpower Alternative* may not fit your needs, but I would suggest they are a good place to start. I think you will find it difficult to find a person who follows what has been suggested as a behavioral model for love would not experience continuous improvement.

Well-Directed Minds Are Principled

To start this conversation, the mind needs to accept that being fully human consumes verbal and nonverbal information in the same way that faith does. We can be fully human when our awakened nonverbal soul is present, and that happens more often when we have a principled objective that includes verbal "willful mercy" direction. Thus, a well-directed mind that lives in truth, not rationalizing self-gratification or being judgmental of others' motives, is primed to stimulate just objectives and live in continuous improvement.

How do we direct our mind to such lofty objectives? By staying focused on the objective principles, not the specifics. For example, if I love someone and become attached, I want my attachment to be for the greater good of the one I love. If my emotional ego has feelings that are not in the best interest of the one I love, I need to see the truth of this hypocrisy because it is not focused on my principled objective. It is like a child who loves their parent and feels attached but does something bad, and they feel remorse for their bad conduct. We do not get up in the morning wanting to be disagreeable. It is the hypocrisy from my lack of truthfulness about the specifics that I often do not have any control of that derails my objective. "In truth- It is what it is." Be willful; have mercy. The proclivity of this Reflexpower from my soul is gratitude.

The good news is Reflexpower is a simple behavioral mechanistic term that requires no effort on my part. And that is a good thing because my effort is encumbered by my judgmental biases and ego causing me to do what I do not want to do. Thus, it is imperative that I give my command, *step aside*, and *willfully* accept the product of my Reflexpower. The objective is to "disarm conflict," regardless of the subject matter, so that I live life on life's terms. I am the master of my domain when I have a well-directed mind. Conflict is nonproductive emotional current that needs redirection by the mind with auditory commands.

The reason conflict can be destructive is that my emotional ego may seek revenge or be judgmental and can easily feel bitterness when challenged by conflict because of past learned experiences, or for some people who have nonconfrontational personalities.

Reflexpower gives us a much-needed, productive reason to *step aside* and allow the process to set us free, by using all the mind's *faculties* to automatically live in peace. This one-step behavioral methodology is very successful when used often because it teaches the mind our preferred objective, stimulating continued improvement, which is *accumulative*, and that, over time, automatically and effortlessly changes *your attitude.* You will find the hardest thing you have to do is to do nothing after giving your command. The command triggers functional fixedness when done often, and your mind amends how it deals with conflict; that alters our attitude, evidenced by no-longer getting angry or having frustration, stress, or anxiety from conflict. Your mind has automatically learned *for you* how to live in peace, and that gets better and better, for more and more objectives, for the rest of your life. How is that for a worthy objective?

The problem that arises for us that none of this will happen until we truly become *willful.* My stumbling block is that I am judgmental, not willful, and that is evidenced every time I give a command and do not passively stand aside, practicing *willfulness*. It is like I said above: *it is hard to do nothing*, but it is absolutely necessary to be willful. Being willful is easy for me. I tell myself I am being willful all the time, but I have deceived myself until I stand aside.

Passively - Stand aside — Have mercy — Reflexpower

It is a little like permanently moving to a country where people speak a different language. That new language has not become your mother tongue until you start dreaming in that adopted language. And this is our willfulness's outcome objective: to subconsciously stand aside or dream in passive terms. This is what amends our attitude about conflict, blazing a path to peace.

You have read almost half of this book, and we have talked much about "Being willful." Integrate how you have judged your behavioral *willfulness* until reading this paragraph. And reevaluate if you have deceived yourself, as I often do, if I do not "Stand aside." What I find scary is asking myself how many times my judgment deceived me when I thought I was being open-minded. *Passively Standing-Aside* when saying these phrases below has been pivotal to me amending my attitude.

- "Living life on life's terms."

- "In truth-It is what it is"

- "Be willful."

- "Have mercy."

Live Life on Life's Terms

Reflexpower™ for Willpower Alternative has an inclusive solution to coping with life's terms. In chapter four, we explain why 90 percent of life's conflicts are out of our sphere of influence, so that leaves us with only 10 percent of our conflict requiring cognitive deliberation. Accepting this one signal reality makes coping with life's terms a manageable task. So how do we get our mind to acknowledge this reality? By giving voice commands to our mind's brain faculties, often until functional fixedness automates nonverbal Reflexpower. The reality of living life on life's terms requires: In truth-It is what it is 90 percent of the time.

It is important we use carefully selected words that convey our true feelings when directing Reflexpower. For example, we cannot use the word "whatever" in place of: In truth-It is what it" because *whatever* is an interrogative word that has no specific meaning or feeling. The phrase "In truth-It is what it is," brings closure to life's terms that are not in our sphere of influence. Using the word *whatever* can easily cause us to actually not care, which is counterproductive to willful cooperation or having mercy.

Much of the 10 percent of life's terms that cause us conflict that is in our sphere of influence can also be handled by giving voice to our preferred nonverbal Reflexpower response, by saying, "Have mercy" or "Be willful," which we have been discussing—hence, an inclusive solution to coping with living life on life's terms.

What does the term "Be willful" mean? I know what you mean by saying, "Have mercy"; you are suggesting I should refrain from harming or punishing others. That is a great question. Saying, "Be willful" is making a very strong statement. For example, when I say, "Be willful—In truth-It is what it is," I am commanding my mind to show a *nonverbal* stubborn and determined intention, *which is a nonverbal Reflexpower factuality* to do as I want, and in this case, it is to accept "It is what it is," regardless of the consequences or effects. Being "willful" is a way for my mind to command my brain to respond with truth "it is what it is and passively stand aside." It changes the proclivity of my mind.

- If the conflict is out of my sphere of influence and I think it is not fair, I am *not* to judge the motives of others.

- If I spill the milk, I accept I am responsible for cleaning up the milk, and I cannot change the fact the milk has been spilled. And being "willful," I should not punish myself.

Likewise, when I say, "Have willful mercy," I am commanding my mind to show a *nonverbal* stubborn and determined intention, which is a nonverbal Reflexpower factuality to do as I want, and in this case, to have mercy, regardless of the consequences or effects. Being "willful" is a way for my mind to command my brain to respond (in this case, to conflict) as if I had *faith* in other human beings to *be fair*, and I am going to refrain from harming or punishing them. By changing the proclivity of my mind, it changes what is at stake: "I should not judge my biases against others; it inhibits impartial judgment." My mind can stay focused on the root cause of the conflict, not my feelings.

- If the conflict is in my sphere or out of my sphere of influence, and I think it is not fair, I am to "be willful" or "have mercy" or "have willful mercy." *Willful mercy* humbles my emotional heart to have the greater good at hand to give my life purposeful objectives that lead me into the satisfaction of achieving continuous improvement.

The outcome is the same; I have become fully human by connecting my cognitive verbal facilities with my awakened nonverbal facilities, and I have mastered the task of having a well-directed mind. When this behavioral strategy becomes the norm and I do it often, functional fixedness sets in, and it becomes effortless, often irresistible.

As an Aside

Most Christian Bibles do not use the words "brain," "emotion," "bias," or "ego" and many other words you just read, because that is modern language. However, the Bible does liberally use the word *love*, some 750 times.

"It is what it is, in truth means passively standing aside," one of the most *unlearned* phrase in the human language, evidenced by our inability to "willfully cooperate" with what we cannot change.

Notes

Chapter Four

Automatic Conflict—Questioning Conflict-Provoking Biases and Practicing Automatic Mercy

September 11, 2001, rattled our nation down to its core values. It was a devastating event that forced a generation of individuals to make sense of senseless mass casualty, but it was also an event that forced that same generation to learn how to prevail above hatred, racism, and defeat.

After 9/11, we gained access to the final moments of many of those who perished that day. Dozens of cell-phone conversations, voice mails, and recorded final moments gave us an insight into what was important to the victims in their final minutes. Many of us are familiar with the phrase "Love others as you love yourself," but I'm sure many of us also believe that this is more of an aspiration than a reality, despite our good intentions. The record we have of that day is proof positive that we are innately good people and that we do, in fact, "love others as we love ourselves." Those faced with certain death did not focus on their imminent fate, their terror, or themselves, but rather spent their final moments telling their loved ones how much they cared for them. This archive shows us that when people are faced with the ultimate sacrifice—their lives—

they come to terms with the fact that the greatest gift of life is selfless love.

Love is the reward we get for living, and love is the reward we leave to those when we are gone. In our waking moments, we should work toward this realization daily so that it comes not only in the final moments of life but in our everyday awareness. We should work on selfless love as a life goal so that it does not become regret. When we do not work to rise above self-absorption, our inaction can turn into regret once we finally feel healing and the powerful harmony of selflessness. When we use every opportunity, we can to do good and to mean well, can regret dwell in any corner of our house?

Cooperation

Life is a little bit like driving a vehicle sometimes. A good driver always enters the car with the intention of driving safely, and a good driver is always aware of one's speed and of being courteous. In order to be a good driver, one needs to cooperate with the rules of the road, conditions of the road, and with the presence of others. After all, driving may seem like a solitary activity, but it's really quite the opposite: we are sharing the road with others always. When we react with road rage, drive aggressively, use cell phones, or drive recklessly (such as when intoxicated), we break our oath as drivers and endanger the lives of those around us. Good drivers are people who realize the privilege and the responsibility they have as operators of a vehicle every time they enter their car.

Just like driving, life is very much about cooperation and about accepting changing conditions and situations with a cool head. When our primary directive is to cooperate and work with others, we accept this as truth, and this changes our biases and our reactions to conflict. After some practice, we realize that cooperating with our selfless soul's spirit is our responsibility as a human being, just as cooperating with other drivers and the road is the responsibility of the driver. When we drive poorly, this can affect our driving record, and when we react to conflict negatively, this can affect our life's mission. Thinking smart about unifying our "heart's emotional nature" by cooperating with our soul's peace-loving mercy allows us to become automatically responsible, and that transforms us for the better.

The Mind's Automatic Processing

The one thing that all humans experience regardless of race, gender, age, and background is emotional currents' Reflexpower. It's a psychological faculty that all brains operate on, and it works best when in conjunction with our spirit's principles and our mind's behavior.

What the methodology of this book seeks to do is to redirect those reflexes through a thoughtful priority: the pursuit of selflessness. When our mind understands that our primary intention in our everyday lives is to cooperate and be selfless, our reflexes can be rerouted in order to get our emotional nature to comply with our intention. However, if our intention is negative or cruel, meaning our behavior and our attitude toward others is combative, unproductive, or unjust, our reflexes will respond in tune.

For example, if our emotional current is emotionally arrogant when we are confronted by a conflict, our brain is influenced by our emotional reflexes such as "fight or flight" and asks our mind, "What is the primary directive?" to which the mind answers, "Satisfy the ego." This then sends the brain the instructions to flick on the negative-reflex switch. When this reflex is set into motion, our body and mind then bring the reflex to its negative conclusion; the process is automatic.

Rerouting our reflexes is much easier than one might think. Because Reflexpower is automatic once learned, I just have to continue sending the positive message "Have mercy" to the brain. When I cooperate by unifying my emotional nature with my soul's goodness, that positive Reflexpower instant response follows. My verbal command has infused my intentions automatically, and I do not have to consider the conflict in front of me; I only have to *consider how I wish to react to it*. Therefore, if something occurs that might usually incite anger or displeasure, the mind has learned from the truth, "it is what it is" and automatically cooperates (which will help resolve the situation) rather than reacting with bias, such as anger (which would only inflame the situation). Try it—it really works. You cannot have two emotions at the same time.

Passively - Stand aside — Have mercy — Reflexpower

Don't Sweat the Small Stuff?

Many of you may be familiar with the hallmark self-help book *Don't Sweat the Small Stuff*, by Richard Carlson.[2] If you are not, the premise can easily be summed up: most of life is made up of situations that we have no control over, and therefore, we have no power to actually solve these issues. Carlson outlines one hundred suggestions in this book alone about how to *deal* with the small stuff, and in his prolific career and in the expansive development of this book series, he probably offers a thousand more. The fact that Carlson has provided reading audiences with such an abundance of advice about the "small stuff" is indicative of how much the "small stuff" can really affect our lives. If there is such a market for this book, many of us are, in fact, preoccupied with finding solutions to life's petty problems or living life on life's terms.

Carlson's approach to this dilemma is that of offering ways to not sweat the small stuff, but I posit that it is much easier to tap into the root of the problem in order to resolve this issue rather than circling around it. Instead of thinking about a million different ways in which we can make the small stuff seem less annoying or frustrating, we can think smart about life's terms.

When we think smart, we ask ourselves the questions, "Can I do anything about this conflict? Or what are my options?" If the answer to the first is no, we need to consider simply cooperating with the situation, and if you want

---

2 Richard Carlson, *Don't Sweat the Small Stuff—and It's All Small Stuff: Simple Ways to Keep the Little Things from Taking Over Your Life* (New York: Hyperion, 1997).

to feel good about doing what is right, do it "willfully by passively standing aside." If the answer is yes, then there is room for compromise if the conflict causes us annoyance.

The majority of conflicts (over 90 percent) that cause us annoyance or resentment are out of our sphere of control. The truth is, *it is what it is.* Be willful; have mercy. Why derail my objectives for something I have no control over? By releasing ourselves of the responsibility or the need to control the conflict, we make it less disturbing to us, as it has been disarmed. Once we adopt a merciful attitude, we can ignore problems that caused us consternation or over which we have no control and instead cooperate with them. In this way, we are truly sowing the seeds of harmony and goodwill, and that stimulates satisfaction with living life on life's terms.

Mercy is a more effective approach than the solutions offered in series such as *Don't Sweat the Small Stuff* because mercy transforms our behavioral attitude with gratitude. Therefore, the small stuff no longer matters, and it makes it easy to accept the loss of that conflict. We have a lot of opportunities to practice being merciful on ourselves, and that helps us hone our faith and behavioral skills because what we do often is what changes our behavior and attitude and brings color to our behavior.

When we see life's terms as a sacrificial loss, this only burdens us with pain and ego. Dwelling on our sacrificial loss to others or to ourselves only gives us frustration, anxiety, and stress. Instead, by changing the foundational pathway with willful cooperation, we can alter life for the better in a meaningful way that gives us peace and joy. We learn to graciously accept our lack of influence on life's terms, and that reality or *truth* gives us freedom.

Planning for Success

At my old job, before I was able to move upward to senior management, I was sent to a seminar on leadership that is attended by many *Fortune* 500 companies and even government organizations. During this seminar, one situation really stood out to me and has lodged itself in my brain ever since. During a talk, a speaker from the Commercial Pilots Association was recalling a common problem experienced in his organization. Many times, dispatchers have a very difficult time talking in-flight pilots out of a problem. Pilots claim that it is difficult to explain the situation to those on the ground, as the experience in the cockpit is not easily conveyable to those not present. While the truth of this statement is probably subjective, one important note the speaker mentioned in closing is that during any type of situation, trivial or grave, it is pivotal to stop for a second and think, "OK, what is my plan?" When we take a minute to examine the situation and our instinctual response to it, we should always ask ourselves, "Do I have a course of action?" and "Does this make sense as a course of action?" Even if the situation is as mundane as going to the grocery store, having a plan or a conception of what needs to get accomplished is important. What happens when you arrive and have not thought about what you need to buy? You may end up frustrated, buying something you might not need, or forgetting something that you meant to purchase.

This can cause a chain reaction of frustration that could have been easily avoided had a plan been formulated. This concept can easily be applied to the small stuff of every day and the big stuff of tomorrow. If we have no plan on how to deal with an issue, we will ignore it, which can be just as bad, if not worse, than reacting to it with immediate resentment.

When we ignore trivial problems, we do not solve them and only create a pressurized and temporary solution that is bound to combust in time. The brain is constantly trying to process the trivial and react to situations and conflicts, and this does not go away until a plan is set up to deal with the information processing effectively. By setting up a plan to reroute Reflexpower by giving voice to our soul by saying, "Have mercy," we are cooperating with conflicts at hand and teaching our minds to get over the bias rather than ignore it or violently react into it. We have constructed *a working plan* toward selflessness rather than allowing ourselves to drift into functional fixedness.

Automatic Behavior in Practice

Picture this: you are in the common area at your job making some coffee. A coworker enters the room, and you pleasantly ask him, "How are you doing? Would you like some coffee?" He walks up to the refrigerator, grabs a water bottle, and mutters, "Nah, I'm fine." Without any further elaboration, he exits the room.

You might be tempted to take this lack of enthusiasm personally; most of us would. You might think, "What's his problem?" or "Jeez, what did I do to deserve that?" The fact is many of us personalize experiences that seem negative. This can lead us to then harbor resentment because we have convinced ourselves to perceive this reaction as a slight. This behavior is what I call a "thoughtless act" because that person may have been preoccupied and unaware of the impact he or she made. The truth is, this behavior may have had nothing to do with us, and our response and resentment is probably being triggered by a previous but similar negative experience.

I can let these situations slide by saying the key phrase, "Have mercy," or by saying positive reaffirming phrases, such as "He did not mean that; it was just a thoughtless act." It's easier to think of what your coworker might be going through instead of jumping to anger. Our soul seeks to be at peace with others. When we give voice to our soul's will by saying, "Be willful," we strengthen our faith when we become unified with the full force of our goodness. Having the humility to put ego aside and cooperate instead can prevent a vague situation from becoming a conflict.

The majority of people we live with and love do not intentionally want us to have resentful feelings about them and usually do not start out meaning to be in conflict with us. We may misspeak or misunderstand each other's intentions, which often triggers unintentional subliminal feelings. It's our primitive emotional nature. This is an inevitability of life, but this is also the reason we should cooperate with others by being flexible and by rerouting our behavior with a positive reflex rather than being resentful. When our minds stay focused on process goals, this mindset gives us the security we need to cooperate with peace. The harmony we receive from this process puts us back in control of the conflict, rather than allowing ourselves to submit to unnecessary resentment and bias. And I should be grateful for my spirit's peace.

Acknowledge your willful soul, and passively stand aside. Does your heart's emotional nature "have mercy" for what you cannot change?

Notes

Chapter Five

Behavioral Truth Model

Last winter, I was visiting with friends who had recently purchased a new home. Although the Pacific Northwest is known for its relatively mild winters, that year an unexpected cold snap drove thousands of Oregonians into their houses for unscheduled hibernation. As I stepped through my friends' front door, I remember feeling the warmth of their well-heated living room embrace my face like a welcoming hug. I sat down on the couch and remarked how inviting the temperature seemed after the cold walk up their driveway. The pair grimaced.

While they were certainly happy about the warmth of their home, their bedroom had become unbearably hot because the furnace was located in the basement right underneath their bedroom floor. They have not slept well during the last few nights; it was obvious that the constant heat had caused them to become cranky and irritable with each other. Because the furnace was unmovable, the couple resigned themselves to two fates: 1) they could either freeze by shutting off the furnace completely, or 2) they could continue dealing with the unbearable heat for the remainder of the winter. Like so many of us, my friends defaulted to all-or-nothing, black-or-white thinking.

I don't know too much about heating and cooling systems, but I knew that there had to be a way to fix their dilemma. I walked into their bedroom, and indeed, it was just as stifling as they had described it. After poking around for a few minutes, I noticed the heat vents that lined the walls were open. I bent down, adjusted the vent so that the panels were in a closed position, and then asked them to wait a few hours to see if they felt a difference.

After dinner, we walked back into the bedroom, and it was noticeably cooler. The heat vents in the remaining other rooms were still open and were circulating enough warmth to keep their bedroom comfortable enough. Their unsolvable problem had suddenly become solved.

My friends are well-educated, professional people, yet their fixed, finite thinking led them to deem this problem unsolvable, which caused them to dwell on the negativity of the situation rather than focus on finding a positive or alternative solution. This is a phenomenon psychologists call "functional fixedness." This classic example will give you an idea of how it works—and a sense of whether you may have fallen into the same trap, one where it is easier to ignore a problem and dwell on the negative rather than to push through in search for the positive. Functional fixedness has nothing to do with intelligence. It can be found in highly intelligent people, as was evidenced in this example.

Yes, it's true that my friends' problem was a seemingly simple one, but we can experience this sort of fixed vision in other important areas of our lives. When I subscribe to this finite thinking, it can impact what is sacred to me and make me unable and, in some cases, unwilling to cooperate with others.

Functional fixedness, however, can be a valuable asset to us when we want to focus on developing a repetitive desirable function, such as Reflexpower. We can do this by giving a voice to our soul's goodness by saying phrases such as "Have mercy" to help us with our attitude when dealing with conflict. When we want to change the proclivity of our emotional nature or cooperate positively, it is good for us to develop functional fixedness. By doing this, we do not have to burden our self-control willpower or become distracted from our behavioral objectives.

Behavioral Objectives

Before we can talk about behavioral objectives, we have to talk about our behavioral deficits. Something that makes human experience universal is that, for most of us, our days can be marred by conflict—whether this takes place in the form of arguments, misunderstandings, or an inability to put oneself in another's shoes.

But from where does conflict arise? And why do so many of us experience it? Let me point you to a common saying: "Do what I say, not what I do." Does that sound familiar? Of course it does. You're probably chuckling because we've all found ourselves in situations where it's relatively easy to dish out advice but fairly difficult to follow your own example. We can call this the vice of infallibility. So what causes us to think of ourselves as being infallible? Is it our black-or-white, right-or-wrong, stiff-necked, rigid, emotional nature that causes it? Why do we find it difficult to negotiate compromise? We will be talking more about this arrogance throughout this chapter.

While many of us would be hesitant to admit to arrogance, it is more pervasive than we sometimes realize. And while an arrogant tendency is not our fault, it is our duty to address it in ourselves. Our greatest asset in unlocking our intelligence and goodness is to acknowledge our spirit's mercy and to interrogate our arrogant denial of our soul's grace. When we deny that we are being arrogant, we are actually being the most arrogant we can be. When our deficits humble us, they become a blessing because that realization can transform us when we are ready to amend our life and our attitude with gratitude. Learning from life's experiences keeps us on a road of continuous improvement, and that is what gives life satisfaction.

So why are we arrogant? What does it mean, and how can we overcome it? We are born with a free mind and a free will, both of which seek to fulfill a need for knowledge. As intelligent beings, we seek out information in order to expand our consciousness and to learn more about the world that surrounds us. Biases, or one-sided perspectives, often accompany the pursuit of knowledge because the temptation to look at a situation from an egocentric heart's emotional nature can lure the best of us. We can look no further than our deeply divided political party system in order to demonstrate bias in practice. By interrogating our arrogance, mental attachment can be switched to our soul, but that requires a fundamental step to disassociate yourself from your ego and biases. When we give voice to our soul by saying, "Be willful" to our executive mind, we disassociate ourselves from our emotional self and strengthen our faith. Our biases can affect much more than the immediate information at hand, they can also expansively impact our ability to cooperate with others and with our intentions.

For many of us, it becomes easy to justify selfish independence or self-importance the more we exercise our free will. The temptation to create universes of which we are the center is strong, and we lose sight of cooperation when our own feelings cloud our judgment. When this happens, our intelligence can become confused and take the back seat. When we let our heart's emotional nature interact with our ego, we can make self-righteous decisions, judgments, and lifestyle choices. This is a normal response because our emotional nature can be self-centered.

For example, how many times have you chastised someone's actions or behavior but have known yourself to behave similarly at one point or another in life? How many times have you sinned or acted out but justified your behavior? How many times have you forgotten what is sacred to your soul in this world and reacted to a situation based on your heart's emotional nature at the moment? In essence, I am asking you, How many times have you let your arrogance control your heart? If you're anything like me, the answer is thousands of times. We pretend to be good people and ignore our hypocrisy, but we end up feeling miserable about our bad behaviors. We become arrogant about our complacency. But it doesn't have to be this way.

When we do things that we hate (i.e., when we are hypocritical), we are living life without a peaceful, selfless purpose, without loving-kindness. We become pretenders, or by another name, we become arrogant. And when we live in arrogance, we are doomed to surround ourselves with negativity. In fact, did you know that scientific studies show that an average person lies at least twenty-five times per day? That is one lie per hour, twenty-four hours per day—twenty-four seven! And that does not count the number of times we lie to ourselves. It has also been proven that we lie more to ourselves than we lie to others. Our lies affect our behavior and character, but they also impact those around us—those we love and those we should learn to love.

So how do we shed our hypocrisy? The most difficult part about adopting and striving toward new behavioral objectives is shedding our attachment to ego. I'm sure many of you are familiar with the concept of ego, but to shed light on how this term will be used in this book, I'll elaborate a bit here. Ego is a human experience to which we chain our minds. Essentially, it is a concept of pride, self-worthiness, or infallibility that some of us, if we're not careful, begin to falsely worship. Catering to our ego prevents us from sharing our life with our soul or others because it grounds us in our reality as we perceive it, and reality is, after all, a highly subjective term.

It is our egos and emotional arrogance that prevent us from becoming humble, cooperating with others, loving peace, and finding true joy through following our soul's principles, rather than our ego's will. And egos can quickly contribute to a sense of arrogance in daily life. Only through the dismissal of our egos will we be able to find satisfaction and unity under our soul's framework for our world. The Bible tells us we are formed after God's own image, which means that we are inherently virtuously good. This is why we feel guilty, bad, or glum when we act hypocritically.

The Behavioral Model: Process

I'd like to spend some time here talking about the process of the behavioral strategy of this book. *Reflexpower™ for Willpower Alternative* uses the idea of *process goals* to achieve *outcome objectives*. Process goals are goals that deal with the process of achieving a big-picture goal, or outcome objective. For example, if my outcome objective is to find new employment, I can focus on process goals, such as applying to five or six jobs a day in order to facilitate my larger goal. Focusing on smaller process goals can help us to secure the bigger picture. In our case, the outcome object that this book focuses on is the achievement of a *well-directed mind that reacts automatically*. Our process goals, which we'll discuss later on, can help us to focus on the larger task at hand.

What exactly do I mean by a well-directed mind? To tackle this question, we must first discuss biases and how they develop. Biases are strong feelings or convictions that arise from experiences, observations, and even fears. Being biased means being limited by a one-sided point of view, lacking a neutral stance, or privileging a prejudiced perspective when the outcome of a situation is not yet known. Our biases are not grounded in objective reality and often are the result of other outcome-based experiences. Quite simply, our biases are grounded in assumption.

In a mind where biases rule, we are constantly faced with opposing thoughts that we give voice and credence to. This process works much like a domino effect. One angry, biased thought often leads to another, irritating the mind and creating conflict that feeds our emotions and our ego. If we do not find a way to help direct our mind out of this hubris in order to process information in a different way, we will *always* find ourselves surrounded by unwanted conflict.

Let's look at the way biases are formed from a different perspective. Scientifically speaking, the sympathetic nervous system (SNS) is one of three parts that make up the autonomic nervous system. The SNS aids in controlling most of the body's internal organs and supports emotions such as stress, resulting in the flight-or-fight reflex. Essentially, the SNS turns emotional switches off and on in your body. How the mind chooses to deal with these switches is where this book can help you to revolutionize the way your mind works. Once a well-directed mind is cultivated, this mind begins to process experiences from a living-life-on-life's-terms perspective because our prejudices, biases, and ego are not involved. Our emotional heart's nature is to be a team player when dealing with information in accordance to my goals and is reflexively cooperative with Reflexpower. Thus, my foundational process goal promotes prompt redirection by saying, "Have mercy."

Many people do not realize that their biases are often expressed by anger or love but not peace. In fact, this is because a majority of us choose not to even think about biases, as it seems there is no methodology available in order to redirect them without considerable effort. Believing that our arrogance or emotions are uncontrollable without a considerable and taxing life effort such as willpower is wrong and is a myth that needs to be broken. We are, in fact, blessed with the ability to redirect our will and intentions. Once our biases and will are redirected, they can inspire us to accept our principles and share goodness with our heart's emotional current. Left undirected, they can poison our behavior and lead to a lifetime of unhappiness and guilt. The choice is yours.

Behavioral Models in Practice

Authentic love's commitment is the highest expression of life we have because it requires us to accept the loss of our judgmentally emotional nature; however, it gives us the greatest satisfaction when we become willfully attached with mercy. Often, selflessness is more difficult to practice than it is to speak about. We cannot purchase humility with money or disingenuous good deeds; it is only when mercy's selflessness becomes effortless that it is in keeping with our principles. In this way, selflessness is applied love. Human reflexes bring into light a new process that provokes instant action without deliberation. *Other behavioral models that aim to instill selflessness do not modulate temperament or interrogate arrogance seamlessly, and are* not *universally achievable in one step.* Below are some examples of other behavioral models that may temporarily or selectively achieve limited results but do not work as universally and seamlessly as this new Reflexpower strategy, which draws our verbal and nonverbal mental resources together.

- Self-talk: The practice of self-talk is rooted in cognitive therapy and requires a practitioner, whether mentally or aloud, to practice talking to oneself positively. It is one of the most widely used forms of "talk therapy" and requires a great deal of strategic thought because it engages with a high-level executive function of the brain. This practice, although helpful to some, is not universal and requires multiple steps to execute.

- Mindfulness: Mindfulness requires a renewed approach to self-talk. The practice centers on awareness of one's self and thoughts, requires high-level strategic thought, and adds a level of emotional control that self-talks lack. This practice is also not universal and requires multiple levels of functioning to execute.

Reflexpower, the behavioral strategy this book is based on, is a methodology that focuses on rerouting conflict with emotional current that stimulates involuntary reflexes. This practice is focused on the use of key phrases and other particular words or phrases to trigger a reflex that is involuntary and predictable, thus allowing us to rewire our behavior in order to act selflessly instead of selfishly. The Reflexpower model counteracts any behavior we have that is fueled by self-centeredness, pretension, or conflict through *emotional current information.* It requires directive thought, which is a low-level activity, allowing us to execute this behavioral model in just one step. This intuitive process is universally predictable and emotionally irresistible.

This behavioral strategy, unlike others before it, finally gives us the tools we need to act upon what is important to us, such as peace and emotional satisfaction in what we love. Through the isolation of "Reflexpower emotional current," we give our executive mind the tools it needs for a well-directed mind. In this way, it is easier to act upon our true intentions, committed love, and willful cooperation, not thoughtless arrogance, which can lead to emotional arrogance. The reason this strategy is exciting is because it augments or automates willpower. Reflexpower allows us to discover our emotional nature's behavior and our biases in a totally new light, one that allows us to rewire our pretenses in order to follow our more virtuous goals. And the possibilities are endless and endlessly gratifying.

Acknowledge your willful soul, not your emotional arrogance. Does your heart's emotional nature have a passion to "cooperate" with an open, willful mind?

Notes

Chapter Six

Human Reflexes

One year, my old college friend Griffin called to tell us that he would like to stop by on his next trip to Portland, Oregon, but that he wouldn't be able to arrive until about 2:00 a.m. I told him that this wasn't a problem and that we would leave the key to the front door in a designated spot for him. Before we hung up, I tried to explain that the new front entry door was a little tricky, as it was installed recently and still had a few kinks. Griffin immediately cut me short and said, "Bill, I know how to open a door." Now, Griffin is an engineer and has always been a little competitive, so I simply responded with, "Great. We look forward to seeing you for breakfast."

Let's flash-forward to the night of Griffin's arrival. Shirley and I are sound asleep when, at 2:30 a.m., we hear a rap on the door. Griffin is outside, and of course, he is having trouble getting the door open. Griffin is a smart person, probably one of the smartest people I've ever had the pleasure of knowing, but his inability to listen and cooperate demonstrates this book's thesis on reflexes. Griffin, like many of us, has been given a key (his, in this case, was literal), but because of his stubbornness or functional fixedness and ego, he was not able to use the simple trick that was required in order to make the lock work. Many of you are probably chuckling at this scenario, and many of you are probably also knowingly nodding—we are all guilty of this kind of behavior because reflexes and biases are hard to stop once they have been initiated.

We may all have biases and a sense of ego, but, as I hope this anecdote demonstrates, it's worth putting them aside in order to cooperate and learn from others' and life's experiences.

The Electrical/Chemical Mechanics of Behavioral Reflexes

I have mentioned a number of times that "what we do often changes us," and this is true. In life, once we are on a path, we tend to follow it for better or worse, and we tend to accept this behavior because we do not understand the basic mechanics of the brain. In this behavioral model, we have unveiled some of the mysteries that kept us from amending life. Reflexive emotional current may seem like a cerebral process, but reflexes are actually an electrical/chemical response to the nervous system faculties. When we are cruel, act badly, lie, hurt others, or privilege our ego, we are moving ourselves further away from our mission by doing what we do not want to do. What we do *often*, for better or worse, can cause the system's faculties to become functionally fixed. This automatic behavior is what makes us creatures of habit.

When we take the time to acknowledge that the mind uses reflexes to direct the brain, that the two operating spheres of our brain are trained by experience, and that the fMRI proves this to us, we are able to see life and ourselves with a new empirical clarity. Therefore, doesn't it make sense that we have to disarm and reroute this system in order to disengage from a reflex geared toward conflict to a reflex geared toward harmony and peace? Yes, it does.

With two operating systems (right and left brain), the mind has a tangible influence upon the brain and commanding authority over it. This gives us the ability to orchestrate our intentions and rewrite our biases at will with executive reasoning. Observing how we naturally can toggle back and forth in between two brain operating systems with reflexes becomes self-evident once we acknowledge that we have the capability to do so!

The Hardwired Truth about Emotional Nature: Learning to Consent with the Conscience

I'd like to spend some time talking about emotional nature and internal conflict. Many of us are born with an innate sense of mercy, but some of us have to work on it. For many of us, the joy of peaceful loving-kindness is a complicated matter, at least in part. While our soul's conscience guides us toward mercy, the contrarian nature of being a human often presents problems in the application of our goals. We may want to act a certain way, yet our biases and ingrained reflexes cause us to react in a contrary way. Humans are infinitely complex, and this makes our actions, reactions, and deliberations more complicated, especially when our hardwired reactions are not compatible with our internal motivations. This application is another example of giving our soul a voice by saying "be willful" to cooperate with our principles and faith. Without my mind consenting to my soul's voice, I cannot have peaceful unity with my primitive heart's emotional current.

When we choose to act on our emotional nature by allowing our biases to reign, we are not engaging our dual-operating spheres and not choosing to consent to internal unification. Instead, we are resigning ourselves to the fixed thought of having one processing system. Our emotional nature is hardwired, meaning it will always be there, like an elephant in the room. Our brain feels hardwired to react a certain way based on these proclivities. While it may be impossible to change our basic nature, what we have control over is the way we choose to respond to it— we have the power to consent to peaceful goodness, to our goals, and to our verbal redirections and reflexes. When we target negative conflict by diffusing our reactions using key phrases such as "Have mercy" or "I am good with that," we are able to divert our response and transform our mode of thinking. What we are essentially doing here is issuing an ultimatum to the self: we are refusing to engage in conflict, and we are choosing to consent with our new behavioral model and our behavioral goal. And in this way, we have created a philosophical awareness of the self.

For example, imagine you and your spouse are on a vacation that requires a lot of driving and limited access to basic services. You have mapped out rest stops where there will be available amenities such as telephones, internet, and gas, and you have shared this itinerary with your spouse. However, your spouse, who is also driving, forgets to make a crucial turn at the predetermined stop, leaving

Passively - Stand aside — Have mercy — Reflexpower

you with no opportunity to service the vehicle or to charge your phone, use the internet, or reprogram the GPS, and your supply of gas is at a point of no return. While your hardwired nature might be inclined to react with anger, frustration, and finally fear (because your spouse accidentally ignored all of your hard planning and potentially left you both stranded without any ability to communicate), your conscience knows this is the wrong reaction. You also understand that mistakes are easy to make and are not always deliberate. Using a verbal redirection and saying to yourself, "Have mercy; it's going to be OK," is better than surrendering to your emotions and fear. You need a plan that will require a level, clear head that is not distracted with negative thinking, and that will not happen until you gain control of your faculties. This behavioral model will guide you toward making this kind of reaction automatic. The proclivity of Reflexpower from our spirit is gratitude, and that stimulates peace in hope and resourcefulness. It is easy to give up the loss of your emotional nature when your mind has positive direction.

By practicing goodness and actively applying the behavioral model to real-life situations, not only can you avoid unnecessary conflict with situations over which you have no control, but you can also take large steps toward becoming the person you seek to be. So, as the example above illustrates, when our emotional nature is in conflict with our conscience, we are allowing our hardwired responses to take control over our behavior or stimulated fear. However, when we choose to approach conflict in a way that promotes cooperation over confrontation, we allow our hardwiring to silently process in the background while we actively choose to respond with harmony. Soon enough, this practice becomes muscle memory, which is the path to automated willpower.

It would be a grave mistake to consider our emotional nature as an expression of our "independent self" because this is exactly what creates a dissonance between who we are and who we want to be. When we are able to reject our emotional current responses toward conflict, we work toward growing into the person we should be: a balanced self who has no need for feeling independence or dissonance. Neither willpower nor patience can push us toward this goal, only Reflexpower's instant response. Once we learn to master our reflexes, it is easier to become a cooperator instead of an agitator. This is the product of a well-directed mind.

The Importance of Every Day

How many times a day do you forget to do something? If you are like most of us, the answer to this question is probably "too many times." But this is a basic fact of human nature: we tend to be forgetful. Whether it's a task on a to-do list that never gets crossed off or forgetting to practice a behavioral change that we've committed to, it can feel hard to fight the battle against everyday absent-mindedness. I'd like to stress that the best way to get over this forgetful tendency is not to bow down in defeat, but to support my effort by saying, "I will do better next time," doubling up on my efforts with positive emotional current.

When we say a key phrase, it gives voice to our mind about our goodness, and that engages reflexes of our choosing. When this becomes our everyday petition, it can evolve into functional fixedness, and you will no longer have to be concerned with forgetfulness.

While we all will forget our life's mission from time to time, it's also important to know that occasional slipups do not equal a relapse. We do not have to be slaves to our mind's rigid operating system; we have the power to change it. Building new pathways for reflexes takes time, and just like muscles instinctively know that their job is to aid walking, this is a learned behavior that becomes automatic. When we practice our goal more, it becomes processed or procedural. For example, Frank Sinatra never thought about how to sing as he was singing, Fred Astaire never thought about how to dance while he was dancing, and Jack Nicklaus didn't think about how to swing a golf club. Their experiences are so ingrained, so practiced, that they have moved beyond deliberation to complex action with no thought required. This is process memory in action, engaging our mental resources to use verbal and nonverbal commands to direct our behavior.

We need to vocalize our intentions. Remember, many things in life may not be within our sphere of control, but rerouting our reflexes and our responses to conflict are goals that are always within reach.

You Need an Attitude Adjustment

It's basic human nature to respond to change with resistance, whether or not that change is imposed internally or externally. The reason for this is that the proposed change is challenging our biases and our view of the world as we perceive it. Therefore, the first thing to do when attempting a behavioral transformation is to sit down with your attitude and have a frank conversation about developing a willful attitude. Automated Reflexpower instant response has made it easy for us to accept a willful attitude because it stimulates functional fixedness for that which we do often.

Question: How do we get ourselves to think with humility? Answer: By questioning our motives for how we behave and what we say. Without that contrarian inquiry, we come to believe our mind instead of the heart of our spirit. Having a caring attitude that cooperates with our soul and others is what it takes to become. When we don't work to adjust our attitudes toward cooperation, we are left with a faulty GPS. You have programmed your destination, but the GPS needs to be able to recalculate and alter your route if you make a wrong turn. A bad attitude is somewhat like a GPS telling me I made a wrong turn over and over again, instead of redirecting me onto an alternative route. We need a willful attitude that supports the mission, not the moment.

By amending our emotional nature's behavioral attitude to be in concert with our soul, we solidify our *hope's* intentions. Actions are louder than words, to our mind and others. It is much easier to stimulate action through automated Reflexpower than it is to debate the subject with our executive mind. At the end of the day, what changes us is what counts.

Reflex Reactions Review

Reactions are important parts of everyday communication. They have the power to alter not only our feelings but also the feelings of others, so it's important to pay attention to the habits we have formed when it comes to responding to conflict. It is easy to get trapped in functional fixedness, for better or worse. When we respond to conflict with defeating statements such as "You always do that," or by saying "Whatever," we are closing the door to further communication with that person (or ourselves) because we are also reinforcing negative pathways in that person's mind. They will associate us with negative conflict resolution rather than with positive conflict resolution. This kind of association can lead to a lack of communication and understanding. Instead, we can use a positive response that takes the personal feelings out of the reaction—for instance, "I'm sorry that you feel this way." This positive reaction opens the door for further productive conversation to take place while conflict is defused by giving voice to our soul, with our mind saying "Have mercy," reinforcing cooperation and positivity as a peaceful reflex.

Another way we can choose to look at reactions is to take the long-tail view. We have all been so upset by something or someone that our entire day was ruined. We are filled with thoughts of how hurt we are, or how thoughtless someone was, or how frustrating the encounter turned out to be. These negative, lingering reactions poison our mind and create a grander, more dramatic wound than necessary. When we do not cooperate and accept change, we make an investment in our continued resentment. Instead we should aim to invest in our principles and practice loving, peaceful kindness through automated Reflexpower. Using liberating phrases and balancing sentiments such as "They are doing the best they can" or "I'm sure this was not the intention" helps us to combat the disappointment of ego and perception. This is the product of a well-directed mind that lives life peacefully on life's terms rather than enduring life with emotional nature feeding judgmental ego and perceptions.

The acceptance of loss is the beginning of freedom because we no longer have expectations. Disappointment, which grows at the root of all expectation, is something that can only be mastered when we disarm conflict. Our soul's selflessness disarms conflict or sin, and a willful mind no longer sees the loss of emotional arrogance as a painful ordeal because selfishness has been disabled. Unless we take steps to transform our pathways and our reactions, we are doomed to repeat the same pattern because of emotional functional fixedness. Taking the time to intellectually deliberate is time consuming and frustrating with each new situation that may arise. This is why the behavior strategy to use automatic Reflexpower instant response is so effective when seeking harmony within our sphere of control. You do not have to be a mental giant to master your behavior, but you do have to take the first step.

Acknowledge your willful soul, stand aside; when your mind gives voice to your spirit's grace, the proclivity of that Reflexpower is gratitude.

Notes

Chapter Seven

Charmingly Disarming—Controlling Conflict through Thinking Smart

The philosophical adage of the half-empty glass versus the half-full glass is a litmus test for the pessimistic or optimistic proclivity of a person and what they hope for. What we do not realize is that this "proclivity" is really the result of an involuntary reflex from your emotional current that causes us to think about the volume of water in a certain way, and that this reflex is adjustable. The litmus test for our internal motives is revealed when we are either selfish or selfless.

As with the glass of water, if we wish to see it half full—or, in our case, to be humbled rather than arrogant—we must communicate this preferred feeling with our mind by giving voice to our heart and soul emotion by saying, "be willful" to alter their emotional current. Instead of saying or thinking "Why me?" or "I do not have time for this," we just have to remember to use our key phrase, and as quickly as that, we have ensured that the soul and mind are in concert with the heart's emotional current. My soul's willfulness is inspiring my mind to give voice to my soul, acting upon my automatic emotional current.

In truth - It is what it is — Emotional current — Be willful

Willfulness is a preverbal reaction with associated thoughts of goodness to do what is right, or the first thing that comes to mind from our reflexive reactions, physical expressions, or emotional current. (A basic example is red = stop, smoke = fire, and green = go.) For example, by saying "Here we go," this is Reflexpower energizing us into action. These images or concepts are all chained to ingrained ideas that are preverbal associations. Reactive surface language has subliminal meaning that allows the proclivity of our reflex to convey an experience without engaging thought.

This is another example of functional fixedness (discussed in chapter four) when acted upon often. It is helpful to have a key word or phrase that stimulates emotional current to remind the mind about the soul's willfulness. For example, the "half-full/half-empty glass of water" phrase stimulates an automatic involuntary proclivity from emotional current, as mentioned above. Giving my soul a voice with the key phrase "Be willful" stimulates an involuntary reflex without engaging additional thought.

Most of us go through life concerned with conflict. We think of conflict management as learning how to defend ourselves from conflict, or worse, ignoring it all together. Both of these strategies are ineffective at getting to the root of the problem, which is our undirected emotional current. Defending conflict often leads to arrogant responses that favor the protection of the ego and the self rather than the idea of cooperating with another. In this way, we should focus on pleasing our merciful spirit, leading our heart's emotional current to redirecting our Reflexpower about the conflict. Reflexes are defined as "actions performed as a response to a stimulus and without conscious thought." But what does that mean exactly? It means that reflexes are irresistible once activated.

Think back to your doctor office visits. When your doctor administers the patellar reflex exam, he or she uses a tiny hammer called a plexor to test the connection between the nerves in the knee and the information processing system of the brain. If your knee kicks out after the plexor taps it, this means that the information sharing between your brain and your knee is in working order. Your knee's reaction is automatic and irresistible to your body because the pathways of information have been established. In this same way, we can apply the concept of Reflexpower and conflict. If we are to learn how to reroute our perception of conflict so that we respond to it with humility by giving our spirit voice rather than intellect, ego, or *arrogance, we have to learn how to rewire the brain's automatic reaction using the Reflexpower™ Willpower Alternative* methodology.

We must realize that the brain's *operating system* and *programming language* is built upon and responds to emotional current in addition to information or data, not the other way around, even though we usually respond with only information and data. All of our experiences, perceptions, feelings, and memories are mere data that have been uploaded into the brain, processed, and cataloged. The brain is consistently updating and acquiring new information. All of this data, however, is affected by our lived experience, our mind's perception of a given situation, and our ego. All of the mind's perceptions foster feelings, biases, and emotional current reactions, which are transformed back into data and fed back to the brain. The brain then dictates a reaction based on this updated data. If we want to change the way we react to conflict, we need to reroute "emotional current information" via the same highway the brain uses: Reflexpower. Basically, we need to pay attention to our automatic reflex current response.

So, for example, you may have a friend who is a good person. He is open and honest and always helpful when needed. However, you have noticed that he can be very critical of your political leanings, sometimes making comments and other times rolling his eyes in disagreement when you bring up current events. As you observe his reactions to your opinions, you have begun to become annoyed by his behavior because you cannot intellectually process why he believes or stands by something that, to you, is clearly foolish. This incompatibility between your friend's opinion and your opinion begins to create conflict in your feelings. Your brain has created a negative relationship between the data point of "friend" and the data point of "politics," therefore enforcing a bias that has now been uploaded as new information. Now, whenever your friend mentions something that you disagree with, you begin feeling defensive and resentful. This sometimes results in being cruel, snapping, or walking away from the discussion.

While this scenario can seem unsolvable—two people simply have different opinions that have caused them to grow apart—there is a way to solve this situation through information rerouting and Reflexpower emotional current. By using this system for reconciliation, both parties will be able to have a harmonious and healthy relationship. But for now, we will start with the idea of *thinking smart* as a primer to *Reflexpower™ Willpower Alternative* methodology.

Thinking Smart as a Primary Function

The goal is to cooperate with our spirit and with one another. For many of us, it may seem easier at church or when we speak about Christianity objectively, but it is no secret that most of us struggle to remember this goal in our day-to-day interactions. While it's easy to hope that we could go back in time and start again in order to get rid of the biases and resentment that have clouded our lives, our relationships, and even our better judgment, we know this is not possible. So how should we handle life's inevitable displeasures? How do we work on the biases and conflicts we have already developed?

This behavioral model uses Reflexpower to reroute negative habits and thinking patterns. When we *think smart*, we use specific reflex-triggering language to bring ourselves back from conflict and toward cooperation. When we use reflex-triggering language, we remind ourselves verbally to cooperate with our soul by reasserting that it is only through the experience of our spirit's mercy that willful cooperation is made easy. More importantly, it can be a daily, hourly, even minute-by-minute reminder of what our goal in this lifetime is: selflessness that is acted upon with cooperation and often that only requires us to passively stand aside.

So how do liberating cooperative phrases work? They're quite simple. All you have to do is give voice to your spirit.

In truth - It is what it is — Emotional current — Be willful

The system is designed to guide the self's mind back to internal goals through verbal redirection. By asking oneself or telling oneself a series of guiding questions and statements, we can stimulate Reflexpower and reroute negative thoughts or biases through liberating phrases, all of which help us to cooperate with others while defusing our own temporary, subjective, and ultimately arrogant emotional current.

For example, let's say you have been experiencing a strain in your relationship with your mother-in-law. She means well, but sometimes her unsolicited advice rubs you the wrong way, which prompts you to react with anger and annoyance. You try not to say anything because you have respect for her and for your wife, but more and more recently, you feel your annoyance and anger threatening to bubble over. This begins to affect your behavior. When you go over to visit your mother-in-law, you sulk and barely speak. When your wife asks you to take her mother to the grocery store, you dread or avoid the situation. These feelings begin to overwhelm you, and you no longer feel it is possible to go back to a time before the flood.

Maybe this situation sounds familiar to you, or maybe a version of it exists elsewhere in your life and with another person. Simple verbal Reflexpower redirection can help to alleviate situations like this and bring you back on track. You know you want to get along with your mother-in-law because that is the smart way to think about it, and you understand on a deep level that she means well despite her abrasive approach. By simply telling her, "Thank you for your advice; it means a lot to me that you care so much about our lives," you can redirect your bias toward anger with positive reinforcement. This supporting liberating phrase is authentic when you accept "having a willful attitude": "I'm good with my mother-in-law, and while I have to listen, I should not judge her motives. She means well or is doing the best she can, and I will cooperate with my soul's mercy by appreciating all the good she does bring into my life, and it won't hurt me to have mercy."

By redirecting your feelings onto a positive highway through liberating cooperative phrases, eventually your relationships with your mother-in-law will no longer cause anguish or annoyance. You will begin to focus on cooperating with her rather than fighting against her. Treasuring and respecting her well-meaning intentions comes to the forefront, and you will be able to approach a situation, which once brought annoyance, with a renewed sense of vigor and cooperation when you acknowledge that the proclivity of Reflexpower from our soul is gratitude.

As another example: When my wife speaks sharply to me and my feelings are hurt, I can think to myself, "She misspoke. I know she did not wake up with the intention of hurting me." This supporting liberating thought is authentic when you accept that "my spirit is merciful." What can that hurt? What can I learn from this? Is she stressed out? How can I help her? In this way, I am not only becoming selfless, but I am also deepening the bonds of my marriage through an interrogation of my own arrogance. Asking questions that push me to look past my ego can help me to be humble and helpful to others in times of stress or need.

The repeated use of liberating phrases in conjunction with Reflexpower can help manage and even dispel bias, prejudices, and meaningless conflict. Our new bias becomes a positive one; we train our mind to seek cooperation over frustration. Liberating phrases cannot only trigger a pattern of goodwill, but they can also help us gain a better understanding of the world around us by allowing us to cooperate more efficiently and humbly with gratitude.

However, there will always be cases where liberating phrases will guide us toward acceptance instead of immediate understanding. Even if understanding evades you at the moment of potential conflict, use a liberating, stabilizing key phrase to reroute the conflict away from your feelings or your need to control the situation. In these ways, we can learn to share our life with our heart and spirit.

Acknowledge your willful soul, passively stand aside. Is your emotional nature willing to "have mercy" when times are difficult?

Notes

Chapter Eight

Reflexpower for Body Language

Have you ever had an interaction with someone that seemed negative because of their body language? It's easy to take body cues as signs of conflict or negativity because of the sheer fact that the body is so expressive. Why is this? It is because much of our body language is driven by emotional current, with nonverbal Reflexpower. What many of us are unaware of is that body language expresses emotions (anger, fear, disgust, contempt, joy, sadness, surprise). We use our hands to articulate, emphasize, and dramatize; our faces to express happiness, disgust, fear; our arms to hug, to hide, and to avoid interaction. Body language is something we don't spend time deliberating because these primitive emotional expressions are not capable of executive reasoning, and they often misspeak. While we might think that our minds or heart are the ultimate source of emotional nature, our body language expresses emotions and can impact or sway our reactions to conflict, as has been evidenced by Reflexpower. Whether or not we realize it, the messages we convey—or seem to convey—through our physical gestures can often affect our interactions and potentially communicate emotions that we perhaps are not intending to emit. Unlike our mental faculties, we have little ability to deliberate meaning through our body language unless we become conscious of it as a reflex. Intentions can be misconstrued easily, and we have little ability to specify the intricate meanings that our physical reactions stand in for.

Our body language, or our *affect response*, is another means of speaking to our biases and disarming conflict. Our physical responses, such as smiling when we are happy or grimacing when we are annoyed, are physical in nature and relate directly to our sympathetic system because they turn physical exertion on or off. These involuntary physical responses are important because they are perhaps some of the most sophisticated reflexes we have. And they provide us with an additional behavioral tool that can act as a finishing coat of polish for our new behavior objective.

Background

The most basic section of the brain is called the basal ganglia. And it does an important job. The basal ganglia is the part of our brain that we associate with subconscious thought, and it is also where all the behind-the-scenes work happens, such as emotions and Reflexpower. This core section of the brain listens to memory in addition to the spontaneous reflexes from the limbic system. Basically, the limbic system is the foundational part of the brain that is in possession of the largest processing section. Just like a computer has a tower, the basal ganglia does similar work. The affect expressions we just talked about use the limbic system to communicate to the brain and to the mind. For instance, when I smile as an emotional response, my limbic system connects the physical event that just occurred to a memory and an associated emotion. The basal ganglia are behind this magic, and emotions can become cast in concrete by functional fixedness, often making our response irresistible.

Affect expressions can include the following:
- Singing, dancing, humming, chanting, and moaning
- Facial and body language
- Breathing, deep breathing, and sighing
- Laughter and chuckling
- Crying or becoming physically overwhelmed by emotions

Note

Love is not an emotion. The conservative definition of an "emotion" is a facial expression or the like, as discussed in chapter three. Remember, love is an outcome objective that is directed by our heart, soul, and mind faculties.

Our physical reactions to emotional current are the most primal and unique traits of human beings. It is our physical expressions that inspire our biases and spark preverbal thoughts. Think about a situation in which someone's physical reaction to a situation took you off guard or surprised you. Their physical reaction may have seemed odd or inappropriate because in your own personal experiences, you have built up a very strict manual of correlations between emotions and physical gestures that you store in your brain. You may associate sighing with boredom, laughter with happiness, and a frown with disappointment, and maybe this person's physical reaction was at odds with the information in your storehouse. We have to remember that our unique experiences with physicality and emotions are just as the word implies—*unique* to us. And if your definition of emotions did not involve facial expressions and you thought love was an emotion, your specific feeling of love was unique to you. This is why it is always so important to keep this in mind whenever you have an interaction that confuses you or if you are tempted to make a judgment call or assumption about someone based on their body language.

For example, I had an interesting experience with my company's financial vice president a few years ago. As the company's senior vice president, I would have financial discussions with this particular person often, and I found it hard to read his body language. We would have discussions that required elaborate explanation, and he would shake his head up and down in what I thought was agreement, but when asked if he agreed with what had been proposed, he would say from time to time with a straight face that he did not agree. It turns out that he was nodding that he understood the explanation, not because he agreed with it. I soon learned to verbally follow up with him when a proposition was on the table because I began to understand that his body language did not exactly reveal what he was actually thinking or feeling.

Negative Laughter

In order to be aware of the dual nature that laughter can serve, I want to take a historical detour into Robert

Provine's book *Laughter: A Scientific Investigation* in order to explore the more primitive aspects of laughter.[3] In Provine's book, we learn that Thomas Hobbes expanded on Plato and Aristotle's notion that laughter is often times subconsciously associated with superiority. He posits that because humanity is in a constant struggle for power, laughter is a physical emotional affect that is awarded to the victor. Hobbes sees power as a "victorious crowing, the vocal equivalent of a triumphant flamenco dance stomped on the chest of fallen adversaries." I believe that Hobbes is right in this respect. Until we learn to identify this internal conflict, and until we identify that we wish to mirror our internal emotional intentions with our external actions, we automatically assume that when we are laughed at, we are being stomped on or judged. When we learn to rid ourselves of the complex of power and instead experience nonjudgmental laughter, *or the belief that laughter could be nonjudgmental*, it is only then that our output and input of affects can disarm conflict.

Positive, Nonjudgmental Laughter Can Reroute Biases

The opportunity that neither Hobbes nor Provine recognized is that laughter, or even chuckling, can play quite a different role when one accepts the world as it is, rather than how one perceives it to be.

For instance, if someone laughs at me, exhibiting a judgment, I can approach the situation from a nonjudg-

---

3   Robert Provine, *Laughter: A Scientific Investigation* (London: Penguin, 2001).

mental, perspective, chuckle, regain control, and even improve my mood. Basically, my opinion, which otherwise would have been poisoned or soured by my experience, has now become rewritten, effecting my perception of reality and thus Reflexpower. My ability to use affect expression (Reflexpower) for positive rerouting means that it could be used as a powerful tool to do good. Not only can I reverse a potentially tense situation, but I can protect my self-esteem or other emotions while also emitting good, selfless, nonjudgmental vibes from emotional current. Instead of indulging in my biased reflex or response and getting angry, I can regain control, reroute my negative reflex, and appropriate the affect expression for my own positive emotional current.

When we accept affect expressions, such as chuckling, as a means to reroute biased conflict, we open up new opportunities for ourselves to build our faith. Reflexpower has doubled its inventory of commands. I do, however, want to caution you about the use of facial expressions and laughter when dealing with interpersonal relationships. While we may use laughter or chuckling as a way of willfully dealing with a situation, it is also possible, because of the fluid nature of body language, that our actions may be interpreted by others as judgmental or cruel. It is easier not to worry about these things when we are alone, but as humans, we have multiple interpersonal relationships, and therefore, we need to be conscious that this is a possible mode of interpretation.

For instance, thirty-five years ago, I found myself in a crowded airport with my wife. We had a little bit of time to kill before our next departure, so we went to search for some foot relief in the lounge. Of course, many of the seats in the lounging area were occupied, but we finally found a few free seats next to a man who had newspapers spread over the majority of them. When we asked if the chairs were occupied, he replied that he was saving one for his wife. I then pointed out that if the newspapers did not occupy all of the chairs, there would be enough room for not only his wife, but for Shirley and me as well. He begrudgingly moved his papers and began to complain about having to give up the room. Although I felt myself getting angry about the situation and uncomfortable about being bullied by a loud and aggressive individual, I smiled, shook my head, and chuckled in order to bring some levity to the situation. (What am I to do? We needed a seat.) Instead, the bully reacted even more aggressively to my chuckle. He jumped up, threatened us, and shook his fist toward us. I really thought he was going to lose control and allow the confrontation to become physical. Luckily, we were able to avoid anything unpleasant by quickly moving out when a gate change was announced. This experience made an indelible impression upon me: don't laugh—even when it is to yourself—while in a confrontational encounter! The moral of the story is that the appearance of any intimidating affect expressions can actually escalate conflict, even if its internal genesis is of a completely different nature.

However, as long as we apply the use of everyday street smarts, we can see that things like chuckling can have powerful negative effects on people when they see it as a victory laugh, but also that it then stands to reason that laughter is equally capable of acting in a positive fashion.

Facial Expressions

In his book *Human Universal*, Donald E. Brown identifies approximately four hundred specific behaviors that are unchanging across the landscape of humanity.[4] Likewise, we can come to the conclusion that, culture aside, most people have a similar "facial grammar"; their mouths curve upward to form smiles almost always. Our facial expressions are predictable because they are reflective of biases in our basic individual natures. Provine likewise states the same research results in *Laughter: A Scientific Investigation*. His in-depth research goes far beyond our current interests, but let's examine several observations that are applicable to our discussion:

1. Facial expressions typically last 0.5 to 2.5 seconds.

2. An "emotional" reflex can be produced from that expression in only two hundred milliseconds.

What we can learn from these observations is that the mind needs less than half the time that the facial expression is displayed to recognize the emotion and much more time to recognize that the smile is being displayed.

Facial expressions are universal and are part of our biological heritage, and it has been argued that they are hard-

---

[4] Donald Brown, *Human Universal* (New York: McGraw-Hill, 1991).

wired to our emotions and considered one of the most complex human mechanisms. There is a general misconception that all smiles are brought about by happy emotions. Many of us, as previously mentioned, employ affect expressions as a means of disarming conflict or to act as a bridge of forgiveness. How many times have you smiled when you have felt uncomfortable? Or perhaps when you've experienced an embarrassment of some sort? It helps us to trigger a nonjudgmental harmony in our lives while also acting as a coping mechanism.

In many ways, because smiling occurs at a quicker reflex rate than other physical affects, the spontaneous reflex from a smile can be used as a way to disarm conflict. What I mean by this is that when I have the automatic response of smiling when I feel conflicted, that emotional reflex (Reflexpower) defuses negative behavior and gives me the time and temperament to stimulate the desired positive reaction.

A great way to practice smiling for social situations is to also practice smiling on your own. I know this may sound silly at first, but think about for instance how often children laugh—on average, around three hundred times a day versus twenty times for adults. Why is this? When we think about this in tandem with Provine's findings that only 20 percent of our laughter stems from happiness; the other resounding 80 percent comes from a place of curbing anxiety, directing behavior with Reflexpower, or coping with grief, and this makes sense. This means that, on the whole, laughter is generally used as a defuser, both biologically and socially. When we practice laughing and smiling on our own, we finally acknowledge the affect potential of Reflexpower for good. By directing our body language, we trigger our feedback system into not only emitting positive effects but also allowing our brain to balance out our emotions—process them—and only then do we give ourselves the time and space to actually *feel* better.

An Experiment

I have an interesting experiment for you to try when you are alone. Put a big smile on your face and chuckle. Do this twice, and then observe your thoughts. You may be self-conscious and think you look silly, but you've initiated a biofeedback loop that transforms the neurochemical balance in your brain, clearing your mind of thoughts and emotional feelings. This is also useful if you are trying to calm your mind for a meditative exercise, prayer, or yoga. If you drift away from your concentration, an inner smile and another chuckle will bring you back. Deep breathing will also help to keep you on track. The more you practice clearing your mind, the better you get at it, and the more useful you will find meditation and activating concentration. You can only have one emotion at a time, and you are choosing what it is going to be at that moment in time. You have that control, and now that you are aware of Reflexpower, and can put it to good use.

Those of us who use laughter and apply positively practiced effects will benefit from other suggested strategies that help us accept disappointment or circumvent conflict. Effective body language is the most convenient and powerful built-in support system that we have—it allows us to redirect our brain and our emotional body to mirror our objectives. Therefore, when we are more conscious about the ways in which body language is used, this seemingly little thing can aid not only our brain's Reflexpower but also fortify it in the long run. We realize how necessary it is to change if we are to be transformed. Master what matters little to you, and your behavior will change *drastically*. In other words, there is little reason to not change and become transformed.

Acknowledge your willful soul, stand aside. Do you practice using body language to defuse conflict?

Notes

Chapter Nine

Over the Hump and More—Willpower Alternative

One day, I found myself in conversation with a retired pastor who had been a missionary in India. Our conversation concerned God's second greatest commandment, "Love your neighbor as yourself." The pastor asked me, "Bill, are you over the hump?" Confused by the phrasing, I paused for a minute to consider the meaning of this inquiry. I asked myself, "Am I truly selfless? Does the endeavor of being selfless still feel like work to me?" After a few seconds, I quickly realized that I was not, in fact, "over the hump." Yes, it was true that I experienced deep, occasional feelings of compassion but not "mercy." It was also true that the urge to love others and my soul as much as I loved myself was not yet a defining theme in my everyday life. I looked back at the pastor and answered, "I'm still a work in progress. Is it easy to get over the hump?" The pastor smiled back and simply said, "It's easy for those who do it."

I walked away from this conversation with a very important insight, one that directly impacted this book and the Reflexpower behavioral strategy. Being over the hump would mean that my emotional nature would no longer feel a loss when I follow my soul's unconditional mercy. Reflexpower methodology requires me to give voice to my soul's principles by saying, "Be merciful," thus stimulating my mind's conscience about the goodness and peace my soul brings. I am responsible for making a verbal choice, awakening my nonverbal Reflexpower, automating my over-the-hump behavioral attitude. Choosing to have mercy is a smart choice because it amends my judgmental emotional nature's biases. See the "over the hump" example below.

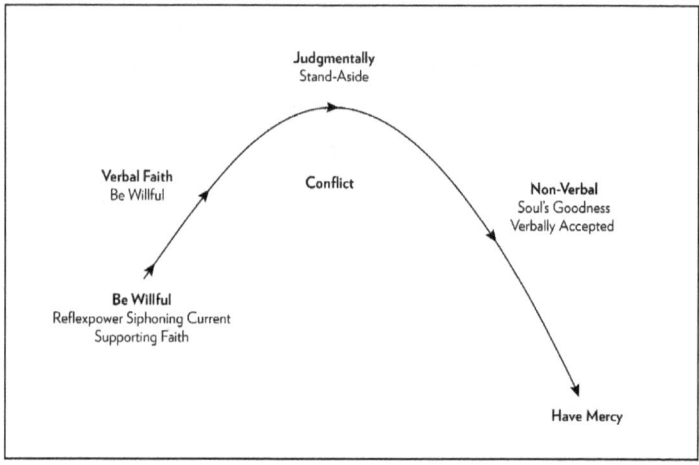

The Reflexpower willful siphon mentally disarms' the *conflict,* and the process is irresistible when you passively stand aside. By utilizing Reflexpower mechanistic faculties you do not have to deal with the conflict, which help us adjust to the mentally reality that 90 percent of all our conflict is out of our sphere of influence. And the remaining 10 percent of conflict that requires deliberate will have a more object outcome. Standing aside and doing nothing requires us to be less judgmental but that is a good thing. When we learn to stand aside often, functional fixedness sets in relieving us of this burden.

This graphic image illustrates Reflexpower new effortless behavioral pathway to peaceful joy.

Self-control willpower may be one of our greatest human strengths that we have, but it has a limited pool of mental resources to draw from, until now. Reflexpower unlocks our mental resources by bringing our *fully human* verbal and awakened nonverbal world together, and this includes our faith-based feelings that bring color to our world.

Knitting the Tapestry of Love: Material Love

As you can imagine, when you have been married for over sixty years, it is not unusual for people to ask, "What's the secret?" Sincere love being a given, my wife, Shirley, and I have come to the conclusion that *mercy* is the secret to a satisfying, long-lasting marriage. Why mercy? Because mercy is the cornerstone to disarming conflict with compassion and prevents you from harming or punishing the one you love, even if unintentionally. When you receive mercy, you feel loved because you have been gifted peaceful understanding. In a marriage, *mercy* is a symbiotic relationship that bonds the marriage together and that makes you feel safe. Loving-kindness is what gratifies our hearts internal goodness. It is about *us*, not *me*, that makes our marriage work. We become one flesh with committed attachment; thus, it is authentic love.

The Soul's Love versus Material Love

Have you ever thought about the difference between the soul's love and material love? If not, it is worth considering. The soul is the incorporeal essence of a human being, for which we should be grateful, and material love is what we empirically experience with continuous improvement. I think it is important to make a distinction between these two types of love because their differences are what make or break authenticity—knowing the difference can help us to work toward cultivating love that stems from both our heart and soul.

When we experience our soul's love, we love with our soul's peace, seeking grace, and our brain's mind appreciates what we love through the lens of humility. We love because we are inspired to do so through our soul's principles rather than being motivated to love by what is in our heart's emotional current, or our mechanical body's lusts. In simplest terms, this means our mind has learned to internalize our spirit's peaceful grace with loving gratitude.

A Word about Compassion, Humility, and Appreciation

Shirley and I have also noticed that having moments of compassion are far different than being constantly inspired to have passion and compassion for others. For example, if your partner spends a lot of time working on a pet project, and you begin to get resentful and feel neglected, this can become a source of conflict. But when you begin to live for your partner, there will be a shift in your thinking that is represented in each and every action of your life and in your interactions together. When you learn to introduce true humility into your lives, your partner's pet project will become a source of joy for you as well. You will encourage their ambition and support their endeavor because their happiness is yours. It is as I said earlier: a marriage becomes one flesh, and that is the reward we get over time. This is a small example of a bigger life goal—true peace.

On the other side of the equation, deep loss can also teach us a thing or two about how invaluable appreciation and compassion can be in our daily lives. Shirley and I lost our seventeen-year-old son in a hiking accident forty-five years ago, and that deep loss spurred an understanding of life's precious moments. What we experienced was an enlightened *appreciation* for that which we lost and an increased sense of understanding and humility in the miracles of every day. If we are to perfect our experience with love as humans, we have to learn how to appreciate every encounter that we possibly can. When we spend too much time being angry about the trivial things in life, or the things we cannot control, our precious time and our opportunity to be compassionate depletes itself like a wasted reserve.

When we exercise Reflexpower, we teach our mind to listen to our nonverbal soul's love, thus redirecting our behavior and expanding our spirit presence. Reflexpower automates the process of overcoming the human habits of annoyance, trivial disappointments, and tics—the everyday conflicts that get in the way of willful cooperation—in order to taste selfless love and to help promote the soul's need for selfless service. Loving-kindness gratifies selfless passion and does not judge the motives of others, and Reflexpower can help hone our soul's passion in dramatic and powerful ways.

The Importance of Self-Love

Many of us struggle with what it means to love and feel loved, and that struggle can affect our everyday interactions and long-term relationships. What arrogance and self-effacement conceal, more often than not, is a much more problematic affair. We criticize ourselves because many of us were taught that self-love is a vain and sinful pursuit. But nothing could be further from the truth.

The reality is that willfulness is being at peace with your soul. If we do not love ourselves at least a little, it becomes very hard to love anyone else, and it becomes even harder to put a behavioral change into motion. Many of our bad habits and hypocrisies stem from a lack of humility and appreciated self-love that includes our soul. When the perfection we expect of ourselves, which seems noble and self-effacing, translates into impossibly high standards we set for the people and world around us, it becomes harder to approach life with humility and selflessness. Conditioning ourselves to think that love is contingent upon a physical or earthly condition (when I lose ten pounds, when I get this job, when I marry this kind of person) makes us lose sight of our relationship with our soul and our appreciation of the soul's gift of mercy. I could not love my wife as fully as possible if I did not love my soul as well. More importantly, as we begin to truly live with mercy and with the aim of fulfilling our soul's true application, we begin to be at peace with our soul from the act of serving others. When we gratify the soul by learning to deflect conflict "In truth-It is what it is," we become a more understanding person, because the truth frees us. When we become humbled by our soul and accept oneself as a manifestation of our soul's image, we infinitely strengthen our relationships with others and the world around in positive, life-affirming gratitude.

Cooperation as an Everyday Labor of Love

As discussed throughout the book, situations over which we have no control can often pose the biggest conflicts and frustrations. It is sometimes easier to be mercifully compassionate or forgiving to your spouse, sibling, or a close friend. When it comes to work situations, new encounters, or strangers, our patience and our egos can easily subvert our desire to be selfless, especially when the consequences of our behaviors and reactions fall to the wayside. Reflexpower behavioral strategy does not discriminate and is not circumstantial: it automatically brings our soul's intentions of selfless love and cooperation into practice and fruition. This model is specifically designed to arouse the power already within us to align our mind with our soul's values and thus cooperate with those around us through good times and bad times.

This section calls willful cooperation a labor of love, but the beauty of nonverbal reflexes lies in the fact that they exist in order to trigger an already preexisting desire for peace and goodness, which, once activated, stimulates our faith to cooperate. Once you begin to cooperate with others instead of feeding conflict, the sweetness of being selfless will inspire your behavior and satisfy your soul. Soon, any behavior that runs counter to mercifulness will feel odd and unsatisfying. When this *transformed* beautiful feeling becomes appreciated, that means your mind has become attached and has passed the hump. Verbal redirections, auto prayers, and body language reflexes will become merely the mechanics behind a much grander master plan.

The Grace of Our Soul Warrants Faith

Learning to incorporate Reflexpower into your long-term behavioral goals will help to achieve the selflessness your soul craves. It is with the utmost importance that we scrutinize ourselves and how our verbal faith consumes our nonverbal soul if our reflexes are to have meaningful longevity and color. As we learn to include our soul's faculties into our everyday behavior, we learn to trust our soul's grace. Willfulness makes it easy to cooperate because nonverbal Reflexpower can put us at peace with what we want to do, not what we hate ourselves for doing, and that builds faith in the behavioral model.

Unifying our judgmental emotional nature with the goodness of our soul's grace solidifies our cooperation with loving-kindness and faith. Experiencing this peace allows us to trust the benefits we develop with faith and color. Losing our emotional arrogance for selflessness is made easy when the benefits give life satisfaction by renewing our faith in doing what is right. What we do often is what changes us and our faith.

Our soul endowed us with free will, and it is our obligation to choose our behavioral action, and we know from experience that is true. When we use Reflexpower to help us do our will, we build our faith in cooperation. Giving our soul a voice by "being willful" does not require deliberation, yet it automatically stimulates reflexes that direct our behavior, which often only requires us to passively stand aside.

Final Thoughts

Through exercising our one-step behavioral model and utilizing Reflexpower, we can grow closer to not only our soul's will but also become unified with our heart's emotional current by becoming more invested in our principles that are in tune with living life on life's terms because "In truth-It is what it is, Passively stand aside." When we come to appreciate the benefits of this *new* behavioral model, we experience effortless transformation.

Reflexpower is merely a means to unlock the goodness already bound within our soul's heart. Reflexes can help us to create a strong bridge between our worldly output and our soul's deepest mercy. The best thing about our reflexes is that when properly stimulated, they can be irresistible and take on repetitive functional fixedness. But most importantly, Reflexpower disarms conflict without emotional loss, paving the way for us to love and, in turn, be loved.

The two main brain faculties we discussed, "heart and mind," help us direct our emotional current and the soul's spirit. By living more through the eyes of the soul's mercy rather than the lens of our emotional currents' biases, we can learn to share our life with our soul. The potential of our soul's goodness far exceeds our emotional currents' proclivities because our soul's spirit is mercy, not our prideful, biased mind and ego. When we become fully human, we are fulfilling our faith's desire to be a decent human who cares about the greater good and is at peace with self and soul, making a difference, doing what we know is the right thing to do.

What keeps us from change is the fear of loss; thus, the acceptance of loss is truly the beginning of freedom. Rejoicing in our loving goodness by giving a voice to our soul's mercy makes it easy to accept the loss of our judgmental, emotional arrogance. Loss is no longer sacrificial when we disarm the conflicts, disabling them from causing us pain.

As an Aside

Sharing the book, *Reflexpower™ for Willpower Alternative,* with the people closest to you, can really help them to understand you as a fully human person and your new behavioral strategy. Without the benefit of reading this information, it would be difficult to follow this advanced understanding of your *new, peaceful* emotional nature. We are all born with a soul's intuitive mercy and can learn from each other's experiences. The greater good from being merciful comes from sharing your goodness with others.

If you are pleased by the book's message, please go online and write a customer review, or post your thoughts online for those you care about. We learn from each other's experiences. Sharing how this technology helped you to improve your quality of life can help others do the same.

Willfulness comes from *faith in self and soul*, freeing us from conflict, putting you at peace with your soul.

Notes

Epilogue

I become fully human when my verbal mind acknowledges my non-verbal soul's spirit, basic emotional nature, and self-seeking body. For Christians, St. Paul, said "yet not I, but the grace of God with me." 1 Corinthians 15:10. Paul's statement establishes the notion we need to use more than our judgmental executive mind to be fully human. When I selectively verbally open facilities such as non-verbal soul's goodness, suppresses my emotional nature, and self-seeking body, re-directing my executive minds biased objectives. Hence, internal conflict becomes manageable. My self-seeking ego's stubbornness which can turn into bitterness has been humbled and the mind can find the strength to "Be willful." This is how you internally disarm the conflict that keeps us from changing our mind. Changing my mind is no longer a un-moveable bias.

The plan for mastering behavioral objectives is to have a well directed mind. My core objective is to *live life on life's terms* with the following goals.—

1. My verbal mind to live at *peace*, with my non-verbal soul, emotional nature, and self-seeking body. Being grateful for this peace brings satisfaction.

2. My behavioral goal is to live life for the greater good of others. Man has no greater love. These goals are achievable by using the following principles.

- Live life in truth, not self-seeking body's selfishness. Then you will know the truth, and the truth will set you free because truth disarms conflict without emotional loss. "In truth-It is what it is."

- Re-direct non-verbal emotional nature's current with truthful Reflexpower of my choosing to control conflict. Re-direction is accumulative when I live by the principle, not living for the moment.

- When I am ready to live in truth, giving voice to my soul's Reflexpower with my verbal mind and faith, stimulates continues improvement.

- When I am confronted with conflict, "Be willful" not judgmental by passively standing aside. I do not have to be judgmental when I am living in truth and we all know that is true because it frees us to "Have mercy."

Getting to know your secret nonverbal soul stimulates our verbal faith, and we become fully human.

Bill Wilson

Prayer of Saint Francis
(Using a Willful Heart and Attitude)

Where there is hatred, a willful heart sows love.

Where there is injury, a willful attitude offers pardon.

Where there is discord, a willful attitude creates harmony.

Where there is falsehood, a willful attitude offers truth.

Where there is doubt, a willful attitude inspires faith.

Where there is despair, a willful heart offers hope.

Where there is shadow, a willful heart brings God's light.

Where there is sadness, a willful heart brings joy.

Action Plan for Prayer of Saint Francis: A *willful attitude* is boosted by the love of a *willful heart*.

Afterwards

Theoretical Summary of the Technology

By Dr. James Lundy

This behavioral model combines the insights of four leading psychiatric theories and techniques: (1) solution-focused therapy, (2) psychodynamic attachment theory, (3) neuroscience and neuroplasticity, and (4) Rogerian communication techniques.

The technology behind the behavioral model finds its origin with Steve de Shazer's insight into solution-focused therapy, namely in the principle of separating the "problem" from the "solution." De Shazer believed that the best therapeutic use of language focused on the surface of what was being said rather than the underlying meaning. He shared this theory with Ludwig Wittgenstein, a leading philosopher of the twentieth century. Wittgenstein believed that attending to the surface of language could solve problems and that our troubles arise when we try to burrow beneath this surface. This perspective separates the problem (and the emotions caused by it) from the solution and keeps the focus entirely on the surface film of language.

This behavioral model's *reflex* strategy expands upon this theory with a specific focus on emotional regulation. Alan Schore, Ph.D., a modern psychoanalytic therapist in the tradition of Freud, sees affective regulation as the essential and main goal of therapy and healthy living. Schore focuses on the neuroscientific research of right brain function (in terms of affect control and the idea that preverbal thought that can be learned and used to exercise healthy self-control). Affective processes appear to lie at the core of self, and due to the intrinsic psychobiological nature of these body-based phenomena, recent models of human development, from infancy throughout the lifespan, are moving toward brain-mind-body conceptualizations. These models are redefining the essential characteristics of what makes us uniquely human.

The technology first separates emotion from problems and uses linguistic techniques to increase emotional regulation and clear thought. It adds to fact that the preverbal affects moderation strategies. After this second tier, it adds a third modality: use of a directive mind over the biological, neuroplastic brain. We are taught that repetition of mind direction will rewire our old, faulty responses with functional responses. Jeffry Schwartz, M.D., at UCLA, has effectively demonstrated both neuroplasticity and mindful self-direction in his groundbreaking research on obsessive compulsive disorder (OCD). His work is the sum total of cognitive behavioral therapy (CBT) and essentially boils it down to a one-step theory of relabeling, and therefore, redirecting.

Lastly, this behavior model draws from *The Conflict of Two Natures* model, which embraces our social and marital world. One of our generation's leading marital therapists, Daniel Wile, Ph.D., teaches us that to effectively communicate with others we must use Carl Rogers's age old technique of empathy in order to learn to speak for the other person. The goal is to trigger conflict resolution by helping the person who you are communicating with to recognize and adjust his or her own affect regulation.

Acknowledgments

I have been working on this book for over a decade with the encouragement of Dr. James Lundy, a practicing psychologist who is also a close friend and our former pastor. Jim's infinite patience with me on this journey and his insightful direction has helped me to understand the process of disarming conflict, stress, and frustration. I owe Jim a great debt of gratitude for his tireless work, support, and friendship these many years. I'd like to thank John, my ghostwriter, who graciously took on the task of explaining this important behavioral process. Because the behavioral model is unique, it required him to actually experience the process in order to put it into words. This book would not have been possible without his talented work and extraordinary effort. I appreciate and value his friendship. Finally, I want to thank my wife, Shirley, for her necessary contribution and patience, and for listening to me talk about and plan this book for over a decade. Shirley is the one whom I learned this behavioral model from, but she did not know it was unique. Those of us who know Shirley know that she is one of a kind. Her personality has most importantly, sincere mercy that uniquely displays trustworthy compassion. Within minutes, people feel totally at ease because of her compassionate behavior. She is my greatest supporter. Shirley, I love you so much.

About the Author

Bill Wilson was a senior vice president for a national paint and industrial chemical company and has been a research fellow for a *Fortune* 500 company. Before retiring in 2000, Bill made a commitment that he was going to become closer to God. He and his wife, Shirley, reside in Portland, Oregon, where they have lived for the past fifty two years and raised their five children.

Examining how to *live life on life's terms* required us to learn how to willfully cooperate with those who are closest to us, which, for Bill, includes God and his wife, Shirley and five children.. Bringing the life of his mind and the life of his soul together only required Bill to think through his life with the help of Shirley, who was blessed with a considerate personality and who chose to build her character with willful mercy. When Bill paused to consider how to cooperate with these sterling qualities, he found how to draw closer to Shirley and others. The fruit of willful *cooperation* inspired him to change his mind and behavior, accepting the loss of selfish control for the 90 percent of things that are not in his sphere of influence, and in that loss, he found the beginning of freedom, and *Reflexpower for Automatic Willpower* was born.

Bibliography

Brown, Donald. *Human Universal.* New York: McGraw-Hill, 1991.

Carlson, Richard. *Don't Sweat the Small Stuff—and It's All Small Stuff: Simple Ways to Keep the Little Things from Taking Over Your Life.* New York: Hyperion, 1997.

Gladwell, Malcolm. *Tipping Point.* Boston: Little Brown, 2000.

Provine, Robert. *Laughter: A Scientific Investigation.* London: Penguin, 2001.

www.ingramcontent.com/pod-product-compliance
Lightning Source LLC
Chambersburg PA
CBHW051402290426
44108CB00015B/2127